About the Author

US Naval Academy graduation photo

Frank G. Tinker was a freelance US pilot who signed up with the Republican forces in Spain because he didn't like Mussolini. He was also attracted by the prospect of adventure and a generous pay cheque. Once over in Spain he took on the bombers and fighter pilots lent to the Fascist rebels by Hitler and Mussolini, who used the Spanish Civil War as a practice ground for the mass bombing of civilian populations. Tinker chalked up the largest number of acknowledged kills with a total of 8 Junkers, Fiats and Messerschmitts. When he returned to the US he was unable to rejoin the Armed Forces and, depressed by Franco's victory, he was found in a hotel room in June 1939 with an empty bottle of whisky by his side and a bullet in his head. This is his account of his experiences in Spain.

SOME STILL LIVE

by

F. G. TINKER, JR.

with an afterword by George Nichols

The Clapton Press

First published by:
Funk & Wagnall's Company, New York and London, 1938

This edition © 2019 The Clapton Press Limited

Afterword © 2019 George Nichols

The Clapton Press Limited
38 Thistlewaite Road
London E5 0QQ

ISBN: 978-1-9996543-8-2

CONTENTS

SOME STILL LIVE

CHAPTER I

OVER THE SPANISH BORDER

When the fighting broke out in Spain in 1936, I was not quite sure which side was fighting for what. I gathered that each was slaughtering the other for being or doing something that the other side did not like. After the heroic defense of the Alcázar at Toledo I was inclined to favor the Rebels. Then came the aerial bombardment of Madrid, and my sympathies swung to the Loyalists. These sympathies increased when I learned that converted Junkers bombers had devastated Madrid. That meant Hitler. Then, when I discovered that Mussolini was taking steps which amounted to a military invasion of Spain, I decided to offer my services as a fighting-plane pilot to the Loyalist Government.

I didn't like Mussolini after Ethiopia. I had tried to volunteer to fly combat planes for Ethiopia in that invasion, but Ethiopia had no representatives in this country and, I found later, had no fighting-planes to fly.

At the time I decided to offer my services I was living in South-eastern Arkansas. I wrote identical letters to the Spanish Ambassador in Washington, the Spanish Consul-General in New York City, and the Spanish Ambassador in Mexico City, giving them my qualifications, which included the Army Flying School course at Randolph Field, Texas, and graduation from the Navy Flying School at Pensacola.

The Spanish Ambassador in Washington wrote that the Government needed no pilots. The Consul-General in New York wrote that he would communicate with me later. But the Ambassador in Mexico City wired me to come at once and sign a contract. I arrived in Mexico City with a Spanish vocabulary of only three words—"*Sí! Sí!*" and "*Caramba*". And I didn't know what the last word meant (N.B. I don't yet). However, two or three of the taxi drivers could speak English, so I hired one of them and went to the hotel he recommended.

The next morning I went to the Spanish embassy and, after identifying myself, was told to return at high noon. I returned a little early, but one of the embassy clerks spied me lounging against a convenient telephone post and invited me to come in and do my waiting inside the building (he didn't know that I never wear a hat and was evidently afraid that I would be sun-struck). After waiting a while longer I was led to an upper and inner chamber where I was interviewed by a gentleman speaking atrocious English. After misunderstanding each other for about twenty minutes I was told to return at 6 o'clock that evening.

When I returned at 6, I had another talk with the same gentleman. We again had a more or less futile engagement until the arrival of a Mexican army officer, who intervened with excellent English. After that we managed to understand each other and our negotiations ended with my signing a contract to fly for the Loyalist Government. I was informed, however, that I would have to travel under a Spanish name and with a Spanish passport. After being instructed to return at 10 o'clock the next morning I set forth for my hotel and, after duly celebrating the new Spanish-American Accord, turned in for the night.

The next morning I showed up right on the dot, but the Mexican army officer failed to arrive. The Ambassador turned up after a dignified diplomatic delay but persisted in lurking coyly in his quarters. The gentleman with the atrocious English, however, acted as a go-between, so I finally managed to understand that I was to have some sort of a mysterious meeting with the embassy clerk at the railroad station at 10 o'clock that night.

Upon keeping this appointment I discovered that there was nothing more mysterious involved than being handed a sealed envelope containing a ticket to New York City and money for traveling expenses. And upon boarding the train I also discovered that the scoundrelly embassy clerk had picked up a little cumshaw by purchasing Pullman tickets for upper berths all the way to New York. This occasioned me no end of trouble, as I had to transact a deal with the conductor every time I changed trains.

The Spanish Consul-General's office in New York questioned me closely, sent me to an American lawyer who was handling these delicate affairs for them, and wished me luck. The lawyer informed me that I was to sail on the *Normandie* for Le Havre at 4 o'clock the following afternoon. When I reported again at his office the next morning, complete with baggage (one suitcase), I saw my Spanish passport for the first time. It informed the world that I was Francisco Gómez Trejo, and that I was a native of the city of Oleiros, in the province of La Coruña. (It was over two months before I learned where the place was, and when I did, it was only to discover that it had been in Franco's hands since the beginning of the war.) I spent fifteen or twenty minutes practising writing my new signature so that I wouldn't absent-mindedly write my real one at the customs desk. I was then given my steamer ticket, baggage stickers, expense money, etc., and set out light-hearted and conscience-free for the pier at which the *Normandie* was lying.

The drama of my adventure began with a comic-opera act—when I convinced the officials that I was only a poor Spaniard trying to get back to the old country. My unmistakable Arkansas accent I explained as follows: my parents had emigrated to Mexico, and one dark night, when I was only two years old, they had sneaked across the border into Texas. Then, a year or so later, they had both inconsiderately died, leaving me to be reared by southern cotton farmers. This also explained my ignorance of the Spanish language. In my later youth I had learned the mechanic's trade by working in various southern garages—the names of which had all been forgotten. I merely wished to return to Spain to rectify the crime my parents had caused me unwittingly to commit by bringing me illegally across the border when I was too young to object. I also wished to see how my aged grandparents, Mr. and Mrs. Gómez and Mr. and Mrs. Trejo, were getting along. I was unable to swear that I had no intention of fighting in Spain, because, for all I knew, I might be drafted and have no choice.

While the customs officials expressed a little incredulity at first, my very evident sincerity soon convinced them that everything was just as I had stated. I almost botched the whole thing when it came to writing my signature, but managed to catch myself just in time. I explained the rather shaky writing by saying that I had thrown a farewell party the night before and, having had a couple of drinks too many, was still a trifle shaky. This statement was, as any of my intimate friends can attest, as near as I came to making an out-and-out false statement. In due course I walked aboard just as though I had a perfect right to do so. However, as soon as I could get to my cabin, I locked myself in, as a further precaution, until after the ship had left the dock. I later found out that this was unnecessary, as I was the only American to leave New York for Spain with a false passport.

Life aboard even a crack liner can become almost unbearably dull, so the various companies provide what they humorously describe as "amusements". In the afternoons there would be movies or band concerts and various deck games. Then at night there would be dances—usually preceded by some such gambling event as a lottery or the rather childish horse race. The best thing I can remember was the Punch and Judy show. It was supposed to be for the children, but they usually had quite a bit of trouble getting in on account of the large number of adults who gathered there every time one of the shows was announced. It was more or less of a relief when we finally arrived at the French Line pier at Le Havre.

The French officials were indifferent to non-Spanish-speaking Spaniards, but let me know what they thought of my brass in coming direct from New York with a phony passport. It seems that the rest of the boys had come from Mexico or had left New York with legal passports which merely stated that they were not valid for travel in Spain.

On New Year's Day I reported to the Spanish agents in Paris and was put aboard a train that night with a ticket to the Spanish border and a pocketful of francs and pesetas. On the train I had the luck to meet the Catalonian Foreign Minister and Agricultural Minister and their interpreter, who had lived in the States for years. Without their assistance I would probably not have been able to get past the French guard at the border.

My Spanish name being Francisco Gómez Trejo, I naturally inferred that Francisco Trejo would be enough of any answer to any questions concerning my name. So when the French customs guard asked for my name (in French) I gave him that answer. It seems, however, that in Spain the middle name is the most important and I should have answered Francisco Gómez. The guard studied my passport and gave every sign of being about to turn me back, when the Catalonian Foreign Minister whispered a few words in his ear. The guard smiled, bowed and allowed me to pass through to the soil of Republican Spain.

With the guards on the Spanish side, of course, I had no trouble at all. They had been told all about me by the Agricultural Minister and the interpreter, so that I was welcomed with open arms. They didn't even inspect my baggage. We took a shuttle train through two or three tunnels to the little Spanish town of Port Bou, six or seven miles away.

We had to wait three or four hours for the next train to Barcelona, so that the Catalonian party took me under their wing and led me out to see the sights of Port Bou. If we had been ordinary travelers we would have been too late for the noon meal, but the august voice of the Foreign Minister had considerable weight in his own province. We were soon informed that our meal was waiting for us at the best tavern in the town. We received a really excellent meal of about six courses, including the best wine I had so far run into, for a cost, in Spanish pesetas, of about thirty cents apiece.

Just as I was about to congratulate myself on what a fine country Spain was going to be to live in, I heard sirens sounding off in the street outside. My new-found friends left the place with an audible swish, leaving me sitting at the table wondering what it was all about. Finally, my slow-moving brain arrived at the conclusion that something might be wrong—so I shambled out into the street just in time to see the hillside across the little harbour erupt into a geyser of assorted dirt and stone. Looking up into the sky, I saw three bi-motored seaplane bombers steaming out in the general direction of the Mediterranean (I afterwards found out that they were headed for the Balearic Islands). Only then did it dawn upon me that I had just seen an unsuccessful attempt to bomb the railroad station at Port Bou.

It was just as well I didn't know what was going on at the time, I suppose, as I would probably have led the parade down to the local bomb shelter—and that would have given my companions a bad impression. Anyway, when they came out of their respective burrows they found me at the table polishing off the remainder of the wine, and my standing and that of *los Estados Unidos* rose. They thought that my staying in the restaurant was due to a disdain for such trivial things as bombs rather than to a dense ignorance of what was going on. At last we heard the Barcelona train coming in, so we went down to the station, which was still in its original condition, and bought our tickets.

The next morning we arrived at Barcelona, where my Catalonian friends were dropping off. Before they left, however, the Agricultural Minister called up a friend of his who could speak good English and put me under his wing, as the minister had doubts as to my ability to purchase tickets from the Spanish ticket agent. It was a very wise move on his part, too, as I found out by a bit of experimenting. The minister's friend arrived just in time to explain that I wasn't having a fit but was merely trying to buy a ticket to Valencia.

At the railroad station I had my first experience with the new Spanish restaurant regulations. I went to the station restaurant and tried to get something to eat, but was informed that only during specified hours could meals be served. Sandwiches, however, could be had with beer at the bar. They only served one sandwich with each beer and as I was very hungry, the situation looked much rosier by the time the train was ready to leave. After ascertaining that neither the conductor nor I could understand each other, I turned in for the night.

When I woke the next morning I got my first glimpse of the scenery in Spain proper, for Catalonia, having its own autonomous government, is not considered (by the Catalonians, anyway) as being Spanish. The usual hills with the same crumbling battlements were in evidence on every hand, so I decided that the movie people haven't been exaggerating, after all. The countryside seemed to be mostly devoted to the raising of grapes and olives, with a few orange groves here and there. Even then the fields were being cultivated by workers—each equipped with either a rifle or a shotgun. And these weapons were either slung about their shoulders or lying close at hand. But even with this evidence of wartime conditions I took time out to wonder at the (to me) strange sight of ripe oranges hanging from trees in January.

Arrived in Valencia, I made the sad discovery that there were no taxicabs available. The Government had taken them all over for use at the front. I had only one suitcase and a handbag, however, and soon hired a porter to lead me to a hotel. The most popular one was the Hotel Inglés so we went there first. No luck—they had a waiting list about a foot long. The next best was the Hotel Regina, where I was very fortunately able to get a small room almost up in the attic.

After cleaning up a bit I went down to the hotel restaurant and made my first acquaintance with real Spanish food. The mainstay of the meal was fish and a plate of small squids with tentacles three or four inches long. I was a little dubious about the squids but, as I would have to get used to the local food, I managed to work up nerve enough to try one and to my great surprise it was really very good. A trifle on the rubbery side, perhaps, but the sauce served with them made them very palatable. Before the waiter got the plate away from me I had polished off all of them. The white wine, too, would have been hard to beat.

My instructions were to report to the Air Ministry, but just as I was leaving the hotel I met a Canadian newspaper representative who informed me that it was absolutely useless to try to see any Spanish official between high noon and 4 o'clock. That was the *siesta* period and it wasn't the custom to do anything during those hours. Therefore we walked around the city until 4 o'clock, and then my friend very kindly showed me to the Air Ministry. It seemed, though, that I was still a little too early, as I was told to return at 7:30 that night and see one of the Air Minister's representatives. There were two very good Spanish-English interpreters at the ministry, so I had no trouble there.

After this interview my friend and I took a walk down to the seaport entrance, where we were turned back by sentries. The port, though rather small, was taking care of a considerable number of ships, most of which had the appearance of food ships.

That evening I reported to the Air Ministry at the appointed time and was ushered into the office of a Spanish aviation officer who was acting as the Air Minister's representative. He could speak English fairly well, but had evidently not had any practice for a number of years. He was unaware of the fact that I had already signed a contract in Mexico City and spent about an hour in very laborious conversation trying to make me understand that they had no particular need for American pilots. However, he said that if I were willing to remain as an officer in the regular Spanish Air Force I was perfectly welcome to do so. This was the only occasion, during all the time I spent in Spain, that any attempt was made to back out of the original agreement. And from the treatment I received afterward I am convinced that this man was acting on his own initiative—with no authority from the Government whatsoever. When he realized that I was already under contract, I was told to return the next day.

When I returned the following morning I found that I was being sent to a flying field near the resort town of Los Alcázares for the purpose of being checked on my ability as a fighter-plane pilot. I was given a safe-conduct certificate and a railroad pass and informed that my train was to leave at 9:30 that night.

All trains leaving Valencia toward the south or to any of the fronts were primarily for military purposes, so that I had to show my identification papers at least three times before I could even get on the train. My officer's pass called for first-class accommodation, so I optimistically located my car and climbed aboard. It was a typical European car, with the passageway on one side and a series of compartments on the other. Each compartment was supposed to accommodate six people, but when I finally located mine there were already seven in it. And all seven were Spaniards, unable to speak a word of any other language. They were all very friendly, however, and after helping me stow my baggage on the overhead rack, made room for me to squeeze in on one of the seats. They tried to make me feel at home by doing their best to open a conversation in Spanish, but it was no use. They talked together for an hour or so and then put out the light and went to sleep.

We reached a little town called Alcázares at 9:30 that morning, and I naturally thought my trip was over—especially when the conductor informed me, among other things, that I was to get off there. However, it seemed that I was only going to change trains there, as it was Los Alcázares that I wanted to go to, and plain Alcázares wouldn't do at all. By that time I was in a muddle, so the conductor put me in charge of the stationmaster and he in turn put me aboard another train about two hours later. The conductor of that train let me ride in peace for about four hours and then grounded me at a little town called Chinchilla. There I found that I would have to wait for about five hours for the train to Los Alcázares. By that time I didn't care much what happened, so I merely sat down and lapsed into a sort of stupor to let time go by as best it might.

Suddenly a burst of rifle fire and the sound of running feet snapped me out of it. By the time I got outside, all the native passengers and loungers had disappeared and the transients were running in and out of the station in aimless terror. I heard the old familiar drone, and almost directly overhead were three bombing planes. As I had a very clear remembrance of what had happened at Port Bou, I dashed over to the outer set of tracks and lay down between the rails. At about that time bombs started falling; fortunately they overshot the station by about 600 feet. Only six bombs were dropped, but they were all big ones. One of them struck a four-story wine factory of heavy stone construction, and all that was left was one corner of the large building.

Two hours later the cause of the bombardment puffed in—two locomotives pulling a long string of freight cars; then, in fifteen minutes, another train exactly like it. That sounds innocent enough, but each car was loaded with a modern tank. And here and there, through each train, was a 50-caliber anti-aircraft machine gun, fully manned and ready for action. I was standing around, dressed in American clothes and looking about as Spanish as an Eskimo, so it wasn't long before an officer from one of the trains came up and asked to see my credentials. My safe-conduct certificate, along with my old reliable passport, completely satisfied him, and I was permitted to continue my gawking. It was good to see this very modern equipment going up to the front for our side.

When my train came chugging in at about 8 o'clock that night I set out for my next port of call. This time my compartment showed signs of having been to the wars. Its windows were broken and its walls were all scarred up by what appeared to be fragments of shrapnel. Its only good point was that it wasn't very crowded. There were only two others in it besides myself and they were both very friendly Spaniards. We were unable to speak to each other, but as they were each equipped with a couple of bottles of fairly good red wine words were unnecessary. We discussed things in general by means of signs, gestures and pictures, but when the conversation ended I'm quite sure that neither side knew what the other side had been talking about. My side didn't, anyway.

A 5 o'clock the next morning the conductor woke me up and I stepped out on the platform at Los Alcázares. Here I ran into another major crisis, as there was only one very sleepy telegraph operator and he couldn't even understand my sign language; but I finally made him understand that I was an American pilot— which seemed to strike some responsive chord in his skull. He talked very rapidly into two different telephones for about ten minutes and then gestured the information to me that everything was all right. And sure enough, about half an hour later a baby Ford showed up and hauled me out to the air station. There it turned out that the officers' quarters were all filled up, so after much arguing between the car driver and the officer of the day I was shown to a room in the sergeants' quarters. By the time, though, I could have slept in the mascot's quarters, if necessary. I then proceeded to get my first real sleep in almost three days.

At the main office the next day I again ran up against the (to me) astounding fact that nothing but Spanish was spoken. My vocabulary, however, had increased, so that I understood almost immediately when I was told to go over to the hotel, eat dinner and then report back to the office. As the hotel was located on the waterfront of the little town just outside of the station, they gave me a guide to make sure that I got there all right.

It turned out to be a typical Spanish building—three stories high—with the usual patio in the center. The dining room was on the side facing the Mediterranean, so it was a very pleasant place to eat. The meal itself, though running more or less to seafood, was also very good, especially after a couple of days' snatching at a bite here and there at railroad stations.

That afternoon I was sent by car to the San Xavier field about nine miles away, where there were three other Americans and one Mexican. The Americans were Harold E. Dahl (who was going under the name of Hernando Diaz Evans), O. D. Bell and Derek Dickenson. The Mexican was an ex-Paraguayan air force commander named Manuel García Gómez. Bell and Dickenson were old-timers of at least forty. Dahl was about twenty-eight, with hair so white that everyone called him Whitey. Manuel was also an old-timer and perhaps the oldest of the lot. He could speak English fairly well and usually acted as interpreter for the rest of us later on.

CHAPTER II

TRYING MY WINGS

San Xavier was one of the finest flying fields in Spain—a large rectangle, perfectly smooth, with an excellent sod surface. There I saw the first of the famous Russian planes which I had heard the Loyalists were using. There were three bombers, nothing more than slightly lighter developments of the Amercian bi-motored Martin bomber and one combat plane, an almost exact replica of the Boeing biplane fighter, P-12. I had had visions of being sent to the front in any kind of old crate.

The next day I had my flight check. A Spanish instructor was to give me a try-out with dual controls, so we climbed into an old Moth for the check. It had been well over a year since I had flown anything and I had my doubts, but the instructor told me to make take-offs and landings, so away we went. After only ten minutes he signaled that he was satisfied. After he got out I took off again for fifteen minutes of solo work and proceeded to have a good time for myself. Flying seems to be something like swimming—once you learn how, you never forget. I tried out all the old stunts and found that they were as easy as ever—needing a little polishing up, true, but no more. When I landed, I was surprised to find that my aerial exhibition had resulted in my being checked out as a certified combat pilot. Manuel told me that I was to go back to Valencia for further instructions—after only twenty-five minutes of aerial work.

Whitey had also checked out that day, so we went over to Los Alcázares together that afternoon. While riding over there I found out why the Air Minister's representative in Valencia had been so surprised when he found out that I had already signed a contract before leaving the States. Whitey and I were the only ones who had contracts—and we had both got them in Mexico. The rest of the boys had come from New York with the promise that they would get them if they could prove that they were fighting-plane pilots. Whitey also told me that there were three other American pilots who had already checked out and had been sent to Valencia. They were Jim Allision, Charlie Koch and A. J. Baumler. All the others except Whitey had come over on the *Normandie* before I did. Whitey was supposed to have made that trip, but he had had a little trouble in Texas on his way up from Mexico City and had had to go back and take a ship to Europe from Vera Cruz. He had got married in Mexico City before leaving and had brought his wife over with him.

Los Alcázares wasn't expecting us and there were no quarters available to us, so Dahl and I returned to San Xavier.

The following day we made another attempt to get away. We hauled our luggage out again and caught a bus to Los Alcázares. This time it seemed that we had forgotten to bring the proper papers along, so back to San Xavier we went. On this trip we took advantage of our ignorance of the Spanish language to get a car for the trip. They wanted to have us return by bus, but we didn't like the busses, so we just never could understand. They would lead us down to the bus stop and very carefully explain when the bus was supposed to come and then leave us there. As soon as they left, we would wander off to the bar and miss the thing—then dash over to the office for further help. After this occurred two or three times they surrendered and gave us a car for the trip.

The next morning we went over to the offices for our papers. Whitey got his all right and left for Los Alcázares. But the commandant at San Xavier thought that twenty-five minutes might be too short a time to judge a pilot's flying ability, so he decided to check me out himself before giving me the required papers. We went out to the field, put on our flying gear and took off in a Polish plane know the Spaniards as the *Cojo-Joven*. It was very similar to the old Navy Corsair, with which I had had considerable experience, and was equipped with an American motor and American-type controls. The commandant told me that the plane could stand anything and intimated that I was to give him the works. Up we went and, after gaining sufficient altitude I gave him my favorite maneuver, a fast loop with a snap roll at the top of it. This turned out to be quite sufficient, because when I looked back I saw the commandant gesticulating violently toward the ground. As soon as we landed he waved me on to Los

Alcázares with his blessing.

That afternoon Whitey and I boarded a Fokker tri-motored transport plane and arrived in Valencia about an hour later. After taking our baggage to the Hotel Inglés we went up to the Air Ministry and presented our credentials. When they had been carefully scrutinized we were instructed to report to the local airdrome at Manises the following day. At the hotel we ran into Allison and Koch, who had already been there several days. The four of us went to the Vodka Café, where we met two or three other Americans, one of them being Sam Brenner. He had come over as an organizer and had turned machine-gunner. From him I learned that besides us Americans there were three or four English pilots in Valencia. As they were on duty at Manises it was very probable that we would all be flying together. He also told me that the only planes they had at Manises were old 1925-model Breguet bombers. I didn't like that very much, because that particular plane had become obsolete almost as soon as the first one came out of the factory.

Manises seemed to be a pretty good field, although certain portions of it were still under construction and workmen were just starting to build a concrete runway on one side of it. When I strolled into the hangar and looked over a couple of Breguets which were under repair I wasn't cheered up by my observations. They were huge crates, with Hispano-Suiza motors, and were equipped to carry a 225-pound bomb under each wing.

I was told to get ready to fly. After drawing a parachute, all I had to do was borrow a helmet and a pair of goggles, which I managed to get from one of the American pilots hanging around. I was to make the first flight with a Spanish pilot who could speak very good English—better English than mine, in fact. Before we took off he said that inasmuch as I had already been checked out as a fighter pilot he would merely sit in the rear cockpit while I took the plane around the field once. After that he would get out and I would be sent up by myself to try the machine out for a while.

Unfortunately, they had been using this particular plane to scatter propaganda sheets behind the enemy's lines and someone had forgotten two or three packages of these sheets—about 1000 in each package—in the plane. Just about the time I started to make my first turn at the end of the field these sheets started coming out—and did they come! The wind would catch them as they came out and plaster them against my face and goggles and hold them there. However, I kept clawing away with my left hand while I flew with my right and finally managed to get the thing down on the ground again. My instructor seemed to be satisfied, though, as he got out and told me to take her up and get a little practice. So I took off with the propaganda sheets still whipping out in my face and took the plane around two more times— making fifteen minutes in all. Then I decided to let well alone and call it a day. When I taxied in to the plane's original location I did my best to make the Spanish mechanic understand what was wrong, but he was still looking puzzled when I left.

The Englishmen and Americans were supposed to form a squadron of Breguet pilots operating from the Manises field. As my contract stipulated that I was to fly any type of military plane I was ordered to fly, that was all right by me.

That afternoon we started practising formation flying. An English pilot, Fairhead, was temporary squadron commander, so he went up first with two wing men. When they had finished, I went up with another English pilot, Loverseed—who acted as patrol leader—and we practised for about an hour. I was flying on the left wing and an Englishman named Papps was holding down the right wing. Loverseed was an excellent pilot, but Papps was sadly lacking in experience. At one time he very nearly ran into the leader's plane and disrupted the entire formation. However, we all managed to land in good shape, so I suppose things might have been worse. In fact, from the conversation I heard later, there was a wild Irish pilot in the first patrol who had done much worse than Papps.

Our flight was the last one of the day. There were two other Americans there—Nolde and Finnick—but when we landed it was so late that they were unable to fly that day. A little Spanish pilot—Barbeitos—came in from Madrid and landed. He had taken some government official there and had arrived just in time to see one of the biggest aerial battles of the year. When he saw what was going on, he cruised around for a while watching the fight—much to the discomfiture of the official.

The Fascists had come over Madrid with a fleet of tri-motored Junkers bombing planes accompanied by a couple of squadrons of Heinkel fighting ships. They had been attacked by four or five squadrons of Russian fighting-planes and had taken a terrible beating. Part of the Russians attacked the Heinkels, while the remainder of them took on the Junkers, diving down upon them in formation. In the resulting melee eleven Junkers and Heinkels were shot down, while only two of the Russian planes were lost. This was cheering news to those of us who expected to fly fighting-planes.

The next morning we found that we were to start flying coast patrol right away. I went out on the southern run—flying formation on a Spanish pilot who was to show me the lay of the land. Under each of my plane wings I had the customary 225-pound bomb by way of offensive armament, and for defense a Spanish rear machine gunner. We inspected several ships but found them to be either ours or neutral, so we returned to the field with nothing to report.

That afternoon the Air Ministry representative came out to the field and gave us a big fight talk, telling us to form any kind of squadron organization we wanted and it would be accepted by the Air Ministry. We immediately held a very formal meeting and proceeded to elect squadron officers. Fairhead was elected squadron commander while I, because of my naval experience, came out with the post of squadron navigator. Though why we needed a navigator to fly up and down a distinct coastline I never could figure out. After reporting the results of our election to the Air Ministry we were further cheered by being told that we were to be given a house of our own—as soon as repairs were completed on it. It was also intimated that more planes and more pilots would soon be forthcoming. All of this we implicitly believed and returned to Valencia feeling very enthusiastic.

One of the most thorough fiascos of the war occurred the next day. We were told that six Breguets were to go up and bomb a little town near Teruel, about 75 miles northwest of Valencia. The expedition was organized in two three-plane V's. A supposedly experienced Spanish pilot was leading the first patrol and

Fairhead was leading the second, of which I was a member. Our escort consisted of three very old Nieuport fighters.

Just before we got there I noticed some sort of commotion about 6000 feet above us and then down came our escort—closely followed by six Italian Fiat fighting-planes. When I looked around again I could see no trace or sign of our first patrol. They had clutched for the ground and headed for home at top speed—about 90 miles an hour. Fairhead having seen none of this, we kept cruising around between a couple of hills near Teruel. His instructions had been to bomb where the first patrol bombed, and with no first patrol he hadn't the slightest idea where to drop our bombs. Why we weren't attacked I have never been able to figure out—I suppose the old saying about the devil looking after his own still holds good. After about fifteen minutes of this we finally headed for home without having dropped a single bomb.

But that wasn't the worst of it. When we arrived at the field, Papps, evidently a little rattled, tried to land downwind, almost ran into a Nieuport coming in from the opposite direction, and crashed. The plane did a complete cartwheel, bombs and all, but fortunately neither one of them exploded. His observer suffered a broken nose and Papps a few minor scratches. The sight of Papp's crash frightened me into making the best landing I had so far made in the "galloping Breguets", as we called them.

When we walked over to the hangar we found that we had been given up for lost when the first patrol came in by itself and reported the Teruel skies as being full of Fiats. All three of our escorting Nieuports and one of their pilots had been riddled with bullets. So our first actual conflict with the enemy ended more or less in their favor. Learning that I was to fly the dawn patrol in the morning, I turned in early.

The dawn patrol was the same as my first one, except that I was by myself and the morning air was considerably cooler. Each patrol lasted over three hours, so they were very effective time killers. That afternoon time was hanging so heavily that I introduced the old Arkansas game of coin-pitching, using, instead of silver dollars, the Spanish five-peseta piece, which is the same size and slightly heavier. In this game two holes, slightly larger than the coins, are dug about twenty feet apart, and the players stand at one hole and toss the coins at the other one. The scoring is the same as in horseshoe pitching: a coin in the hole counts as five points, otherwise the nearest one to the hole counts one point. The first player to reach twenty-five points wins the game.

The game went over astonishingly well with everybody present, including the Spaniards. No sooner would a game start than a huge gallery of spectators would congregate, often becoming so great as to impede the progress of the game. They caught on to the scoring system very quickly and in a short time there were holes being dug all over the airdrome. The game's popularity increased even further when they discovered that it was custom for the winner to get the coin the loser had been using.

At noon the next day we had a bombardment scare: three planes had been seen over Teruel heading in our direction. The sirens began to sound off, and people started walking away from the field into the olive orchards on three sides of us. Two of our trusty Nieuports took off to defend the field, but the enemy, fortunately, failed to appear. The Nieuports flew around for about an hour, and when they returned one of them executed a very pretty ground loop. He even managed to scrape a wing, which is very hard to do, as anyone acquainted with that type of plane can testify.

For the next two or three days we had no flying to do. Why? I don't know. All we had to do was hang around the field all day pitching coins and playing dominoes. I did, however, manage to win enough money from the Irishman to cause him to settle by giving me a very fine pair of American goggles which he had. I used those goggles all the time I was flying in Spain.

On the eighteenth of January I went out on the afternoon coast patrol to the south. We spotted an Italian freighter about two miles at sea and inspected it very closely. In fact, I made two or three approaches over it, in perfect position for bombing. My rear gunner, who also acted as bomber, decided that it was harmless and let it go. However, when we returned to the field a couple of hours later we found a very neat bullet hole through one of our wooden propeller blades.

Two days later I received word to report to the Air Ministry. Upon arriving there I found Allison, Koch and Whitey already waiting. Allison and Koch were busy haggling over contracts. Whitey and I already had ours, but the other two had come over to Spain on the strength of a promise that they would get them later. They did, indeed, get the same contracts that we had, and the four of us left the Ministry with orders to shove off for Los Alcázares on the 9 o'clock train that night. We gathered that we were being sent there to take part in the formation of a new all-Spanish fighting-plane squadron.

When we arrived at the station that night we found that the Mexican pilot, Manuel, was also going with us. As soon as the train started, we also started a poker game which lasted until the small hours of the morning. A considerable number of pesetas changed hands, but not very much real money. The next day we continued the game and managed to pass the time very handily until our arrival in the Los Alcázares station at 9 o'clock that night. Then we all took the bus to San Xavier as usual and started hanging around. That was a mistake, because the commanding officer saw us and decided that we might as well fly one of the old Nieuports by way of becoming accustomed to fighting-planes. What a plane! It had a stick that bore a close resemblance to a section of railroad cross-tie—and the plane itself handled about as easily as an old-time Mack truck.

I flew the thing only half an hour, but that was quite enough. When I came down I made one of the best landings I have ever made. The old crate rolled along for about fifty yards and then—evidently of its own accord—jumped up about ten feet in the air. When it came down, after bouncing violently three or four more times, it started cantering along, first on one wheel and then on the other, somewhat like a frisky pony. I must add, though, that it did roll along almost normally for the last fifty or sixty feet. I got out of it with a feeling of astonishment—caused primarily by the fact that I was still alive and secondarily by the fact that I had found a worse plane than the Breguet.

The next day all of us except Manuel were loaded on a bus and taken to a training field on the other side of Los Alcázares. There we were very pleased to see five sleek-looking biplanes of the

Boeing P-12 type ready for action. We were introduced to our future squadron commander, Captain LaCalle, and then the Russian instructors took charge.

Captain LaCalle was a tall, thin Spaniard, with an unruly mane of very black hair. We found out later that he had an amazing war record. He had shot down no less than eleven German and Italian fighting-planes while flying in Nieuports. He turned out to have the very rare quality of being a natural leader of men, as we found out on several occasions later on. He had been a sergeant in the regular Spanish Air Corps before the war, and had worked his way up to the rank of Captain by sheer merit. He had lately been flying the Boeing fighters with the Russians and had become very popular with them.

Our two Russian instructors were huge fellows, very red-faced, and very efficient. Besides us Americans there were ten or twelve Spanish pilots who were to undergo the same instructions. We were each given at least two flights during the day, and I was tickled to discover that the plane handled almost exactly like the Navy fighter, F-4-B, which had been the last American fighting-plane I had flown.

Some of the Spanish boys made heavy weather out of their first flights, making landings that would have cracked up an ordinary plane. But this plane was one of the strongest I have ever seen and could take an amazing amount of punishment. The Spanish boys had such a limited amount of experience that I thought they did very good work for their first flights in this type of plane. Most of them only needed a little more experience to become excellent pilots. Some of them actually had under fifty hours of total flying time. At the United States Army Flying School the students hardly even see a flighting plane before they have at least 165 hours of flying time in training ships. And even then they manage to crack up a goodly number.

While returning to San Xavier that evening on the bus we four Americans received a great surprise. We had been discussing our future squadron mates among ourselves very loudly, secure in our mistaken belief that none of them could understand English. All at once a rather heavy-set fellow, right behind us, whom we had taken for a Spaniard, started laughing in a startlingly

American fashion. As all four of our heads swiveled around in unison, he remarked, still laughing, "Before you fellows start discussing me, I thought I had better tell you that I am an American, too." His name was Ben Leider, and he had been flying various types of transport planes in Spain for several months. He gave us quite a bit of useful information concerning flying conditions, and we were only too glad to have another American added to our little group.

The following day we had formation practice and two dogfights between different groups. One of the Spanish pilots, who was called *Chato* (snub-nose) on account of his rather flat features, broke two tailskids in succession that day. He had had less experience than any of the others but seemed to be improving very quickly. At the end of the day the Russian in charge asked us Americans if we wanted to form our own patrol or fly spread out among the Spanish pilots. Because Allison was the only one of us who could speak Spanish we decided that we had better stick together. So the patrol was formed with Koch leading, Jim and I flying wing positions, and Whitey flying in No. 4 position. Ben, who could also speak Spanish, had come there with some of the Spanish pilots and decided that he would continue to fly with them. After that second day with the new planes we unanimously decided that they were all right.

The next day we had dogfighting in formation. That was the first time any of us had ever tried it, so we were all rather sorry when time was called about the middle of the afternoon. Fortunately, all of us had more or less experience in formation flying, so we did fairly well. The Spanish lads, though, had a rather tough time of it. Without experience, they scattered all over the sky.

We found out that we had been very highly honored by being assigned to that squadron. It was, as I have already mentioned, the first all-Spanish squadron to be organized in Spain to fly the new fighting-planes. Practically every active Spanish pilot in Loyalist territory was perfectly willing to swap his interest in hell for the privilege of getting into it. All the Spanish pilots who were in training with us had proved themselves on some front or other in either old Nieuport fighters or equally old Breguet bombers.

We also found out why we had been having such a hard time getting assigned to fighting-planes. It seemed that the first batch of American pilots who went to Spain had left us an extremely unsavory reputation to live down. They had arrived in Spain drunk, were drunk practically all the time they were there, and were still drunk when they were poured aboard the homeward bound steamer. Then when they arrived in the States they actually had the gall to say that they had been unfairly treated by the Government. The only thing we regretted was that they had been too fairly treated. With any other government in the world they would all have been lined up against the nearest wall.

CHAPTER III

THE AMERICAN PATROL

Now came machine gun practice. Over on one side of the field they had three large white canvas targets laid out on the ground. We would make our approaches at an altitude of about 3000 feet, go into a steep dive, fire at the target, and then pull out at an altitude of anywhere from 300 to 600 feet. In spite of the fact that Whitey and I had both had previous experience at that sort of thing, our final scores were rather embarrassing. It was all new to Jim and Charlie Koch, but they did as well as we did. After we had each made two passes at the target we were sent up for a little more formation practice. On this day we laid the foundation for a reputation which spread throughout Spanish aviation circles—the reputation that Americans are the world's best formation pilots. We were all feeling in particularly fine fettle and managed to fly in almost perfect formation, holding our positions in practically every aerial maneuver that has ever been thought of. So we went home that evening feeling very well pleased with ourselves and passed the time away by playing poker—after locating Manuel to play the fifth hand.

The next day we received still another form of training—firing at a sleeve target towed by another plane. This practice also helped to convince Whitey and me that we were both terribly rusty with machine guns. Neither one of us hit the sleeve more than three or four times. In between our passes we would go up and practise formation flying. With each flight we could feel ourselves slipping more and more into our old flying form. We had all been entirely out of touch with aviation for at least a year and needed all the practice we could get. I was especially rusty, due to the fact that my last year of flying had been done in the Navy, where a good tea room stance is of more importance than flying ability.

The following day we had some more machine gun practice, but about noon the wind increased to such a velocity that all flying was called off for the day. We caught the bus and went back to San Xavier. We arrived there just in time to see a belated Breguet coming in—at the same time that a small cyclone also came in. The unfortunate Breguet came to a complete stop and then, when it turned to taxi in to the ramp, the wind got under one of its wings and turned it over on its back. The pilot, however, was uninjured. At about the same time a British training plane (a Fleet) came in, bounced a couple of times, and then very gracefully stood up on its nose. After hanging around in the field until there was no possibility of seeing any other accidents we went over to our quarters and started the usual poker game. In all these games we were using Spanish pesetas so that, although a great deal of money changed hands, it never amounted to very much in American money (or "real money", as we called it).

The next morning Charlie Koch was sick in bed with severe stomach pains. The sudden shift from American to Spanish food had finally got him down. All of us had been having more or less trouble trying to get used to the excessive amounts of olive oil served with the food. Jim, Whitey, and I escorted him over to the station hospital and then went to the training field. It was very windy that day, too, but our Russian chief instructor decided that it wasn't too rough for flying, so up we went. This time we fired at the ground targets while flying in formation—with Jim leading the formation in Charlie's place and with Whitey and me flying the wing positions.

We wound up the day by having a violent check flight, with the San Xavier station commander, Major Sampil, leading the formation; and he really put himself out, too. As all three of us managed to stick to him, we were all checked out and informed that we had successfully completed the training course. We were also told that we would leave for Murcia the next day, where we would be given new Russian fighting-planes to take to the front with us.

Charlie was allowed to walk over to the station to see us off. He was almost broken-hearted at being left behind, and we were feeling just as badly at having to leave with only three-fourths of our original American patrol. We were rather fortunate, however, in having another pilot named "Chang" Selles ready to take his

32

place. He was called Chang because he had been born and reared in Japan and could speak Japanese, English and Spanish with equal fluency. The only drawback to his English was that he had evidently learned it from English tutors and had also acquired the English sense of humor (or lack of it). At any rate, he never could see the point of our jokes without mulling them over. It was startling to hear him burst into idiotic laughter long after we had forgotten the joke. We became great friends, and he remained in our patrol as long as it lasted.

Captain LaCalle was waiting for us at Murcia. He had all pilots up in his room that night and gave us a fight talk, translated by Chang. LaCalle brought out some very good champagne and we drank to the success of the new squadron. It was remarkable how he could inspire others with enthusiasm, even when his words had to be translated.

The next morning we were hauled out to the local military airdrome at Alcantarilla, where we looked over our new planes and met our future mechanics. The fuselage and wings of my plane had been manufactured in Russia and the motor was a brand-new Wright Cyclone manufactured in Paterson, New Jersey. My mechanic was a huge and near-sighted Asturian named Chamorro—and I still couldn't roll my double r's. We spent the rest of the morning climbing around over the planes and adjusting our parachute and cockpit straps. We were all pleased to note that the parachutes were very reliable ones of American manufacture. After the noon meal we took off and got a little squadron formation practice, which didn't turn out as well as it might have. The leader of the third patrol was one of the new Spanish pilots, and this was his first experience in squadron formation. He was either entirely or almost lost on practically every maneuver. At the end of this flight each of us received a complimentary flying outfit—leather trousers, flying jacket, fur-lined boots, helmet and gloves. I had been in Spain one month.

On February second, LaCalle sent *La Patrulla Americana*, as we were called, out for a fifty-minute period of formation practice. Jim, as usual, was leading, Whitey and I were flying the wing positions, and Ben and Chang were bringing up the rear. This was an experiment on LaCalle's part, as a five-plane patrol was unheard of. The five-plane formation turned out to be much more cumbersome to handle. When we came in, Chang made a violent landing and stood his plane up on its nose. This put the plane out of commission for the time being, not to mention the extreme embarrassment it caused Chang.

That afternoon we were inspected by both the Spanish and the Russian Air Chiefs. Then we gave them an exhibition five-plane formation flight. LaCalle himself led this flight, with Jim, Whitey and myself, and a Spanish pilot (Berthial) flying on the wings. This formation didn't turn out so well, mostly on account of the sudden shift in leadership and the fact that we were all flying in strange positions. Every patrol leader has different mannerisms which have to be learned by his wing men, and the change from Jim to LaCalle threw all of us a little out of synchronization. The ground observers, though, seemed to think that we had done extremely well and showered us with congratulations.

The wind kept us on the ground the next day. LaCalle sent us Americans out to stand by our planes as a sort of guard patrol. It was extremely hot in the sun and dust, and we finally rigged up a canvas plane cover as a windbreaker and started a game of hearts at five pesetas a game. A kindly old farmer came over from a house near the field with a pitcher of cool wine. We liked it so much that we bought three more bottles from him. When relieved, we went into the local village to eat and had more wine. When we could just barely see straight, we received word that we were to leave for Albacete as soon as possible.

Whitey immediately decided to call up his wife, who was at the Hotel Inglés in Valencia, and tell her the good news. So he wandered off in search of a phone booth while the rest of us went down the street to a café to have our coffee and cognac. When the bus came after us there was still no sign of Whitey. Jim and I stalled around as long as we could and then, both of us very popped, climbed on top of the bus and started out for the field. After the bus had traveled about 200 yards down the street Jim shouted down to LaCalle that Whitey was missing. LaCalle had the bus stopped at once and ordered out a searching party. Jim and I, eager to help, both fell off the top of the bus, bounced a couple of times, and went dashing back in the direction we had come from. But all our efforts were unavailing—there was no Whitey to be found. So we finally climbed back aboard the bus and continued our trip to the field.

When we arrived at the airdrome we all went out to our planes to await the starting signal—a red rocket fired into the air from a Very pistol. After Jim and I had sat around mourning for about ten minutes, Whitey came tearing up in a private car, quite sure that he was going to be too late—and quite as popped as we were. We sat around for about ten more minutes and then, still having seen no starting signal, we decided that our threatened departure was a false alarm. So we propositioned the kindly old farmer for more bottles of his excellent wine and resumed our game of hearts. Just as we finished the second bottle we heard a dull detonation, and a red rocked soared into the air from the control tower. By that time we could hardly see the foot-high numbers painted on the sides of the planes.

Anyway, we had our planes cranked up and away we went. After I had climbed about 1600 feet my motor started sputtering and finally stopped completely, so I turned 180 degrees to the left and made a dead-stick landing, stopping right in the middle of the field I had just left. When the emergency crew came out, the chief mechanic pointed out the reason why my motor had stopped. I had accidentally pushed the altitude control lever all the way forward, thus cutting off the gas supply. With a very red face I again had the plane cranked up and took off.

The flight we made to Albacete was, in itself, a proof that military pilots have charmed lives. The three of us were so full of wine that we wouldn't have care if the entire enemy air force had come over and attacked us. Whitey and I decided that this would be a very appropriate time to demonstrate how formation should be flown. We would close in on Jim's plane so closely that at least twice he had to reach out and push our wings away from his cockpit. Then we would practise changing positions. In other words, one of us would slide over, while the other was sliding under, Jim's plane. It was only a matter of luck that we happened to select opposite sides in these latter maneuvers, as we had no prearranged signals.

When we arrived over the field at Albacete I succeeded in

committing one of the major crimes in Spanish aviation circles—
landing before the squadron commander. The cause of this was
that I peered over the side and saw a huge white landing Tee on
the ground below. To my muddled brain a Tee meant a landing
field and a landing field meant a landing. So down I went—and
executed a perfect landing about five minutes before LaCalle
even got in position to come in for his landing. When he did get
down on the ground, though, he broke into the finest display of
Spanish oratorical fireworks that I have ever had the pleasure of
hearing. Practically every word and every gesture in the language
was used before he finished his tirade, which at some points
seemed to indicate that I was to face a firing squad before sunset.
Fortunately, I could understand hardly a word he said, so my
feelings were practically unruffled when he got through.

The worst, however, was yet to come. When we were hauled
up to the ramp in front of the hangar we found a reception
committee waiting for us. There were representatives from the
various political parties, with a generous sprinkling of colonels
and generals. And each of those people seemed to think that he
would be shirking his duty to the cause if he made a speech of
less than fifteen minutes in length. The only good thing we could
find about this procedure was that we couldn't understand a
word they were saying. During all this time we were standing at
attention, out in the hot sun, and thinking very unflattering
thoughts about people who kept poor tired aviators on their feet
after flying hours. An occasional very audible hiccough from the
American patrol didn't help.

Good old Captain LaCalle was merely waiting for the dust to
settle before he went to work on me in particular and the
American patrol in general. He called poor old Jim over and told
him he was to act as interpreter—Chang was still at Alcantarilla
waiting for his plane to be repaired. Then he went at the three of
us in earnest.

It seemed that our conduct previous to the take-off had been
accepted by LaCalle and the rest of the Spanish pilots as nothing
more than typical American horseplay. But when we started
playing our funny stuff in the air and then wound up with the
exhibition in front of the populace of Albacete, we had gone too

far. He wished he could believe we were too weak-minded to know any better. Jim finally managed to convince him that Americans always pulled off such tricks when on their way to the front. He had served in the World War, so he was considered an authority. Anyway, we finally got off with being warned not to let it occur again.

When LaCalle finished his tirade, we were piled into a bus and taken into Albacete proper. The accommodations at the hotel weren't so good—for me and Jim, anyway. We drew an inside room with no windows and an transom that wouldn't open. But the meals were the worst trial—they were positively saturated with olive oil, and the principal course was usually fish of some sort. The cooking, of course, was usually very good, but we Americans just weren't used to the unusual amounts of olive oil. We finally solved the problem by eating nothing but eggs. These were fried or scrambled in olive oil, but we could hold them up on a fork for a few seconds and let most of it drain off. Even at that, our American stomachs were in more or less of an aching condition for a couple of hours after each meal. And the high percentage of oil, of course, necessitated at least three or four trips into the underbrush per day.

Fortunately, we got back into LaCalle's good graces the next day. He detailed us to give a demonstration of acrobatic formation flying for the benefit of the delegation before which we had disgraced him. We had been flying together long enough now to know each other's flying characteristics by heart, so we really put on a show. We started off by doing vertical climbing banks—"lazy eights" in technical parlance—dives, zooms and diving spirals, all in tight V formation. After that came a few steep chandelles and a couple of loops—still in the same formation. Then we closed the show by shifting the formation into echelon and landing right in front of our spectators. Our landing was a little ragged, but it was evidently the best ever seen in those parts. When we motored in to the ramp LaCalle was beaming with pride and still being congratulated by the goggle-eyed political representatives.

The thing we got the biggest kick out of, though, was the way our mechanics acted. They had been lording it all over the mechanics of the other patrols because their pilots couldn't fly formation as well as the American pilots. After our demonstration flight they were almost impossible for the other mechanics to live with. We could hear them jeering at the others during meal hours (by this time my Spanish had advanced to the stage where I could at least understand that jeering was being done). We were afraid that their overbearing conduct would get us in bad with the Spanish pilots but discovered, to our amazement, that they were just as proud of us as our own mechanics were. Their viewpoint was that our performance had reflected credit on the whole squadron. Even their mechanics did a little bragging about us when our own mechanics weren't with them.

Jim awoke on February fifth with a very bad cold and was hardly able to speak above a whisper. On this particular morning we were due to have a practice dogfight with a squadron of Russian pilots who had just come back from the Madrid front. The purpose was to give us experience in the aerial tactics actually being used at the front. Jim insisted on taking part.

We met the "enemy" over a prearranged spot. After our first attack in patrol formation we broke up and engaged them in individual combat. I picked out one of their planes and we made head-on passes at each other for about fifteen minutes before I finally tried one of my own maneuvers and ended up with him on my tail—so I was theoretically shot down. Jim was also shot down, but Whitey managed to get behind his man and followed him all over the sky. After the fight, which lasted about fifty minutes, we landed and waited for our recent adversaries to come over from their field. Then we went to the field café and talked things over with them. There we losers were told by the Russian pilots what mistakes we had made and just why we had been shot down.

My adversary, with whom I had had a very active half-hour, told me my flying had been perfectly all right up until my final maneuver. Then I had made the fatal mistake of diving instead of climbing. He seemed to be a pretty nice fellow and as we both knew about the same amount of Spanish we got along fine. Our technical conversation was carried on through an interpreter, but after that the two squadrons sat around and exchanged bad Spanish, concluding by piling into a bus for Albacete and a night club, where we celebrated in proper style. Jim's cold, however, was so much worse that the squadron doctor ordered him to bed as soon as we got to town.

At sunset the next day we learned that the whole squadron was to leave for the Madrid front the following morning. We hurried in to tell Jim—whom we found greatly improved. Part of his improvement was no doubt due to the fact that he had just received a telegram from his wife's family in Mexico to the effect that he was the father of a fine baby boy. However he wasn't sufficiently recovered to celebrate the occasion, so Whitey, Ben and I had nothing else to do but go to bed.

The next morning Jim was on the field, taking no chance of getting left behind. A huge Douglas transport plane was to carry our mechanics and our luggage to the front, so as soon as they were loaded we all took off and headed for the flying field at Guadalajara, about thirty miles northeast of Madrid. We were supposed to have a field of our own, but heavy rains had left our field too muddy to use. The Douglas led the way while we, in squadron formation, flew protection over the tail.

Just as we were flying over the last mountain before reaching Guadalajara, LaCalle gave the signal to shift over into the right echelon. His left wing man, Chato Castenedo, immediately proceeded to swing under LaCalle's plane, and at the same time Ben, who was flying the right-wing position, hit an air pocket and went down, causing the two planes to collide in mid air. Chato's propeller cut off Ben's right tire and chewed up part of his fuselage and lower right wing, but they managed to separate. Chato's plane was not damaged at all, but Ben's was in pretty bad shape. His long experience as a commercial pilot stood him in good stead and he made one of the best "dead-stick" one-wheel landings I have ever seen.

The field at Guadalajara is a long, narrow, triangular field which can be landed on from only two directions. Ben circled around over it until the rest of us had landed. By that time, of course, we all knew that he was going to take to his parachute and let the plane get down as best it could. We could see from the ground that his right wheel was completely wrecked and that his lower right wing was just barely hanging on. When we saw him start making practice approaches to the field we all thought he was practically committing suicide. However, he finally set her down—left wing low—and when the speed started to fall off, he went into a controlled ground loop to the right. The centrifugal force caused by this maneuver balanced the plane on the left wheel as long as possible, and when the right wheel finally touched the ground it was going so slowly that it just barely went up on its nose before falling back again. The only damage done in the landing was to one of the propeller blades, which was bent.

At Guadalajara we found ten sleek-looking monoplane fighters. They were almost exact copies of our American Army fighters of the P-26 type. The only difference was that they had retractable landing gear, were better streamlined, and had more powerful motors. Experienced Russian pilots were flying them. If we were good boys throughout the war we might be allowed to fly these planes after the armistice was signed. LaCalle told us this as we were motoring to the field house.

CHAPTER IV

UNDER FIRE AT GUADALAJARA

Madrid's triangular flying field lies just across the Henares River from the city of Guadalajara, which is the capital of the province of the same name. The Madrid-Zaragoza railroad was on our side of the river and ran along the eastern long side of our field. This combination of an important flying field and an important railroad was a favorite target for the Fascist bombers. In fact, it had also been a target for the Government bombers when the Fascists were in possession of the city at the outset of the war. Between the railroad station and the short side of the field was what had been an assembly plant of the Hispano-Suiza Automobile Company. These buildings had been completely wrecked by showers of light and heavy aerial bombs and, from the air, presented the most war torn sight that I saw anywhere in Spain. The nearby field had also been the target for many of the night bombardments and was covered with filled-in bomb craters.

A large building at the southeast corner of the field had been converted into a field house for the use of the aviation personnel. A huge carpet, very thick, and some rich draperies had been taken from the palace of a local duke and installed there for our benefit. There were also long dining tables and several smaller tables for gaming purposes. It was to this building that we were taken when we first arrived, and it was there that we met the members of the Russian squadron. All were using Spanish names. The Russian commander, Captain Ramón, was especially interested in us Americans. I fear, however, that we hurt his feelings in the conversation we had after the noon meal.

Ramón and several others gathered around Jim, Whitey, Ben and me. The Russians had been there only a little more than two months, so their knowledge of Spanish was about as limited as ours. Both sides depended on an interpreter. At first we merely asked them about flying conditions in that vicinity and answered questions about flying conditions in the States. Then the conversation shifted to the monoplanes we had seen in the field. LaCalle had already told us how slim our chances were of ever flying them, so we took no pains to get on the good side of the Russians. The conversation jogged along somewhat as follows— allowing for misunderstandings due to interpretation:

RAMÓN: Have you ever seen planes like those before?
JIM: *Segurísimamente.* (Why, certainly).
WHITEY: Hell, yes. (Whitey had actually flown our American P-26 model while in the American Army).
MYSELF: Sí, Sí. (My Spanish was still a bit weak).
RAMÓN: (Looking slightly surprised): Do you think that you could fly them?
WHITEY: Oh, I flew planes like this about three years ago.
RAMÓN: (Looking astonished): What?
JIM: Yeah, they're a little antiquated, but I suppose we could learn to fly the things again.

At this Ramón, the interpreter and the other Russians went into a heated huddle with themselves; they were probably making sure that the interpreter had heard and translated aright. Then Ramón came back into the fray:

RAMÓN: These planes are the most modern fighting-planes in the world.
THE THREE OF US: Aw, boloney (or its equivalent); we've seen the same things in the United States at least five years ago.
ALL RUSSIANS: !*#%&@-#*$&%****! (may be translated as general disbelief).

Ramón appealed to the interpreter for moral support, but was informed that our argument was technically correct—that the original model of those planes—minus developments—had come out in the United States at least four years before. This precipitated a private quarrel which almost ended in blows, and the interpreter stomped off in a huff. We were thus left with no means of making ourselves understood to each other, so things were left dangling as they were.

We went out to the local hotel in Guadalajara that night and were assigned to temporary quarters. It was a large building about four stories high and Whitey, Jim and I had the bad luck to draw a room up on the top floor. Ben was in a room just across the way with LaCalle's other two wing men, Chato and Calderón. Chang was still in Albacete waiting for his plane to be repaired, so our patrol occupied an entire room. LaCalle, who was in a room on the floor below with Ramón, came around to see how we were getting along and told us we would be moved to permanent quarters near our other field as soon as it dried up enough to be used. It was a brand new field and the continual rains had made a regular morass out of it.

Speaking of continual rains—they really have them in Spain. The Russians said they hadn't been able to fly for over two weeks. For the next two days all we had to do was sit around in the field house and listen to the clatter of the rain on its tin roof. The only variation was when it started hailing or sleeting. The clouds would get so low that quite often the neighboring hilltops would be hidden. The Henares River marks the eastern boundary of the Guadalajara Valley, so that there is a line of hills and plateaus all along its eastern bank. Occasionally we could see the dull loom of the Sierra Guadarrama off to the northwest, but usually there was nothing but lead-colored clouds and sheets of rain to be seen in that direction. We were naturally interested in the Sierra Guadarrama because we had been warned to stay this side of it if we got lost, as its crest marked the line between Government and Rebel territory.

It was during these long dreary days that we pilots really learned to know each other, to appreciate one another, and to recognize little peculiarities and idiosyncrasies. LaCalle was tall, rather slightly built, with weather-beaten features and a shock of raven-black hair which stood straight up whenever he took his helmet off—which was seldom. He was all business when flying, but in times of leisure was almost boyish. As squadron commander he had a car and chauffeur for his own use, and he had picked out the tiniest car I have ever seen. There was hardly room in the thing for him and his chauffeur at the same time. His favorite wet-weather pastime was driving furiously over the wet field and skidding round and round. He also played with a motorcycle and a couple of bicycles every time he got a chance. His chauffeur had one of the easiest jobs in Spain, because LaCalle invariably drove the car himself. He would also argue on any and all subjects, and had the Spanish trait of furiously waving his hands and arms while arguing.

Jim was a typical Texan, the tallest man in the squadron—with a carefully tended mustache—and the best storyteller. He was an old-timer and had flown practically everything that could fly. Part of his flying career had been spent in the Navy, and another part had evidently been in the liquor trade during the prohibition era. He had married a girl in Mexico a year or so before coming to Spain, so he was pretty well brushed up on his Spanish. He had an apparently unlimited supply of the latest jokes and had the knack of getting them off in a way no one else could. I can see him now, sprawled out in an easy chair in front of the stove reeling off one of his yarns.

Whitey Dahl was the one of us who stood out most prominently when among Spaniards. He and I were exactly the same height—five feet eleven—but he was considerably heavier. I weighed about 165 pounds and was considered a big man by the Spaniard, but Whitey must have tipped the scales at pretty close to 200. His florid complexion and extremely blond hair and eyebrows were striking in Spain. The difference in his voice and manner of speaking also made him stand out. He had the Midwesterner's boisterous way of speaking, while Jim and I both had our southern drawl and accent. Whitey's favorite occupation was writing letters to his wife, who was then in Paris. His infatuation with his wife was a constant source of wonder to the Spaniards. They couldn't imagine why one should continue to be in such a state after marriage.

Ben was the serious-minded one of our American group. He was the shortest, but was so solidly built that this went unnoticed. He was a member of the Communist Party and would sometimes give us very comprehensive talks on world politics. I wasn't a member of any party, but I would frequently get into arguments with Ben over the social system down South. He invariably won the arguments. He was much admired by the rest of us for the fact that, with no previous military training, he had volunteered for duty in fighting-planes.

All of us were on excellent terms with our Spanish flying mates and soon learned to recognize our names with their Spanish pronunciations. Jim was "Jeem", Ben was "Lando" (his *nom de guerre*), and Whitey was naturally "Rubio", the Spanish for blond. I was "Trejo"—pronounced *tray-ho*—because that was the name on my passport, although later the Russians insisted on calling me "Francisco". This was because they considered it more comradely to call one by the first name than by the last.

Chang was still in Albacete. He was the runt, being only five feet four. The flying suits were all the same size, and were just about right for Whitey and me; but Chang was completely lost in his outfit and was a source of amusement whenever he appeared in it. He was a great favorite with everyone, and his perfect knowledge of both Spanish and English made him almost indispensable to us later on when we started flying reconnaissance flights. Some of our orders were so complicated that we was the only one who could interpret them. He could also speak Japanese perfectly, and people were always asking him to show them how their names looked in Japanese.

These days of inactivity came in rather handy, after all. What time we didn't spend in talking to each other we spent playing cards or dominoes. LaCalle had very wisely placed a ban on gambling, so all the games were of a social character. We taught the Spaniards how to play hearts and poker, and were in turn taught how to play their games. The Spaniards had a different system of playing dominoes, and the Russians taught us a very complicated card game which they were constantly playing.

February tenth was a big day for us—on that day we made our first flights over enemy territory. Although the rain had stopped it was very cloudy and just barely fit for flying.

Our planes had bomb racks which could hold four twenty-five-pound bombs. After the bombs had been loaded in the racks, each pilot checked over the plane and tested his bomb release. Then we were given a look at our objective on a large military map which LaCalle brought around to each patrol. Our first mission was to bomb two powder factories just across the Jarama River about fifteen miles southeast of Madrid. LaCalle very carefully explained what we were to do, what formation we were to use, and how we could recognize our targets best. Then we were told to stand by our planes and wait for the starting signal—a white flare fired into the air from the field house. As soon as LaCalle finished his rounds and got back to his plane the rocket was fired and off we went.

At this time the ceiling had lifted to about 3000 feet, making it easy to sneak across the front line under cover of the clouds. LaCalle knew that particular part of the country by heart and got us into perfect position slightly beyond our objective. We were in the formation known as a V or V's. In other words, the planes of each patrol were in V formation and the patrols themselves were flying in V formation on LaCalle's patrol. LaCalle turned the formation until we were headed back toward our own territory and then, when we were almost directly over the two factories, he gave the attack signal and down we went—still in the same formation. LaCalle's patrol was to take the anti-aircraft battery, which was known to be located between the two factories, and each of the wing patrols was to take the factory on its side.

The maneuver worked exceedingly well. We carefully lined up our bomb sights and, after steadying down on the target, released our bombs. Then we continued on in the dive and machine-gunned the little figures we could see madly scurrying around in the factory yards. We then flattened out in the dive and utilized our excess speed in zipping across the Jarama River. As soon as we got back into our own territory we flew as close to the ground as we could, using any valleys and draws which happened to be handy, so that enemy observers couldn't see which direction we departed in.

That afternoon we made another trip over the line and bombed the same two factories again, also throwing in the usual machine-gun fire. On this trip we were very thoroughly bored by anti-aircraft fire. At the same time, though, no one but LaCalle knew that it was anti-aircraft fire, so we thought nothing of it. The shells they were firing at were leaving white puffs of smoke, and inasmuch as the clouds we were diving through were white cumulus we thought that the shell bursts were little detached clouds. Such is the bliss of ignorance. LaCalle was the only one who had to do any worrying.

The formation we were using on these flights probably sounds a little complicated and cumbersome, but it really was just the opposite. Whenever we made a turn in either direction the American patrol would cross over LaCalle's patrol and the No. 3 patrol would slide under. By using these tactics the entire squadron could make turns almost as quickly as one patrol could make them by itself.

On these two first flights our formation didn't hold together as well as it might have after our dives. I think this was caused by the fact that we were all trying to see what happened when our bombs hit the ground. LaCalle bawled out the American patrol because we had also strafed the enemy trenches on the way back. He told us that it was a useless risk of both our lives and the planes. We explained that since we had to pass over the enemy trenches anyway we though we might just as well strafe them. LaCalle warned us not to let it happen again, scowling officially all the time; but I think he was just a little proud of our exhibition. He in particular, and the rest of us in general, were warmly congratulated. It seemed that three monoplanes had been sent out to check up on our activities and had seen the whole show. On our last flight we had seen them coming in, which was the first time we had seen any of them in action. They certainly looked wicked when they were up in the air. With their wheels up, they were very little more than a wing, a motor and two machine guns. Each machine gun, though, had a volume of fire of about 1800 bullets per minute, so when both trips were pressed about 3600 bullets per minute were sprayed in the direction the plane was heading. That was almost as great a volume of fire as we had with our four machine guns.

They came into the field after we did, so we had the pleasure of watching them land. They were certainly an improvement over our own American monoplane fighter which I had seen at Randolph Field some two or three years before. Their landing gear was especially remarkable. The wheels were about two feet farther apart and much stronger than those of the American model. The field at Guadalajara was very rough, and although these planes landed at a speed around 100 miles per hour, I saw no wheels carry away. We resolved that we would do our best to get to fly them before we left Spain. It so happened, however, that I was the only member of our little group to have that pleasure.

The enemy also seemed to think well of our work, because they came over that night and bombed the countryside. They didn't even come near to Guadalajara, though, and some of the explosions were so far off as to be barely audible. However, this was our first night bombardment scare, so it was rather interesting.

First we heard rifles popping away, out near the edge of the town, and then a siren sounded the general alarm. We gazed questioningly at LaCalle, who merely shrugged his shoulders and remarked, "Junkers—*aparatos fascistas*" (Junkers—Fascist bombers). He further remarked that the siren was the signal for us to go to the *refugio* (bomb shelter), but that there was really no need of hurrying until the lights were turned out all over the city. So we all sauntered out into the street just as the lights were turned out and were shown to the nearest *refugio*.

Our *refugio* turned out to be an old wine cellar, with new side passages which had been dug out to increase its capacity. Besides ourselves it contained all the civilian population of that area of the city, including many women and children. They seemed to be perfectly accustomed to that sort of thing and were all chattering away at a great rate when we got there. Candles had been lighted in niches in the dirt walls, and the general atmosphere of the place was more like that of a social gathering than of a life-and-death affair. We pilots took advantage with some of the local *señoritas* whom we had seen walking about the streets at other times. Several of the Spanish boys produced the inevitable goatskin wine containers—from which wine is squirted, at a sanitary distance, into the mouth—and we passed a very pleasant couple of hours before unanimously decided that the enemies had taken their playthings home for the night.

The following day we made two more trips into enemy territory. This time we had instructions to bomb and machine-gun enemy artillery emplacements just over the Jarama River from the little town of Aranjuez. We were also given orders to come back over a certain bridge which enemy troops were trying to capture and see what we could do to them. On our first trip we noticed that there was quite a bit of anti-aircraft fire, but they didn't register any hits, so we came back with an even worse opinion of their effectiveness. On the second trip, though, our opinion of them was raised considerably when they made a direct hit on one of the planes in LaCalle's patrol.

His patrol went down first, and as our patrol came down to about 1600 feet behind him we had an impressive view of the entire affair. Eight bursts of white anti-aircraft puffs appeared, about 300 feet ahead of LaCalle's patrol, but they were making about 300 miles per hour in an almost vertical dive, so there was nothing they could do except keep on going. The next group of white puffs boxed the group almost perfectly, and one of the shells evidently made a direct hit on the gas tank of the left wing man's plane. The plane blew up with a terrific explosion in mid-air, in a huge cloud of black smoke, leaving nothing in sight except a few wing and tail fragments slowly drifting down. Our American patrol managed to swerve to the right—we had already dropped our bombs—and went into a series of dodging evolutions which got us over into our own territory safely. Then we went over to the bridge and took it out on the Rebel troops who were trying to capture it. When we got back to the field we discovered that one of our best Spanish pilots, José Calderón, had been the occupant of the destroyed plane. He had been LaCalle's best friend and boon companion. The only consolation we could offer him was that Calderón had undoubtedly been killed instantaneously.

This was the first life contributed by our squadron, and it affected us deeply. There had already been so much slaughter in Spain, however, that the Spanish boys were accustomed to losing a friend or a relative at any time. When we offered our condolences they merely shrugged their shoulders and murmured, "*Es la guerra.*" They moped around for a while, looking downcast, but soon regained their usual gay spirits.

CHAPTER V

BATTLE IN THE CLOUDS

Shortly after we landed, Chang came in from Albacete with his newly-repaired plane, so we had four planes in our American patrol once again. He arrived just in time to help us discover from LaCalle that we were to move over to our own private field—Campo X—that afternoon. As it was only about nine miles away we were hardly off the ground before we had to land again. The field was still a little too wet in places for flying purposes, as the leader of the third patrol, Berthial, found out to his embarrassment. He made a perfect landing, but just before his plane stopped rolling his wheels sank hub-deep in the mud, causing the plane to turn slowly up on its nose. The only damage, however, was a bent propeller blade, and that was soon exchanged for another.

We also found that we were to change our living quarters from the hotel in Guadalajara to a house in a little town near our new field. The name of the town was Azuqueca, and it was some time before I was able to pronounce it properly. Our new field, incidentally, had been part of the country estate of a former count. His country home was over near one corner of the field and was a typical aristocratic country establishment. It was in the form of a huge square with an old-fashioned arch-covered gate leading into the patio. The count's home formed one complete side of the square, and the quarters for his retainers were built around the other sides. The militiamen who guarded our field lived in these retainers' quarters. The authorities evidently considered the necks of pilots and mechanics too valuable to risk near a flying field at night.

That night we had our evening meal in the main dining room of the count's house. It was a beautiful room, complete with all its original furniture and silverware. The long dining table had been lengthened even a bit more, so that there was room enough for both pilots and mechanics to eat at the same table; the reason for this became apparent at the end of the meal. The meal itself was very good, but there was a little too much olive oil in it to suit us Americans. The end of the meal was indicated by the service of coffee and cognac. Then LaCalle rapped on the table for attention and gave us a violent harangue in Spanish. At one point he made some statements which were the signal for all of the mechanics to jump up and start talking—or rather, yelling—in unison. We discovered, through Chang, that he had just informed them that they were to eat at a table in the next room while only pilots and the Russian technical advisers were to eat in the principal dining room, in which we were at that time.

It was then that we discovered, to our amazement, that all the mechanics were commissioned officers, while some of the pilots were still non-commissioned officers. In our United States flying units the mechanics are always non-commissioned officers and the pilots are almost invariably commissioned officers; and even if not commissioned, they always hold a rating superior to that of their mechanics. But in the Air Force of the People's Army in Spain all promotion on both the mechanics' and the pilots' branches is attained either by length of service or by deeds of valor. Take Chang's case, for instance; he was a sergeant pilot, while his mechanic held a first lieutenant's commission. In fact, my own mechanic, Chamorro, also was a first lieutenant, while I was theoretically only a second lieutenant. What the mechanics had taken offense at was what they thought to be an intimation by LaCalle that they, commissioned officers, weren't good enough to eat at the same table with pilots, some of whom were non-commissioned officers.

The discussion was broken up by a telephone call informing us that enemy night bombers were headed in our direction. We immediately set out for the open countryside in busses. The bus I was in got as far as the main highway—about a quarter of a mile away from the field—when we heard the motors droning overhead. The bus was stopped at once and we all took to the comfortably deep ditch alongside the road. We had hardly got settled down in the ditch when one of the night raiders laid a line of small demolition bombs down the far side of our new field— almost as accurately as though it had been broad daylight instead of 10 o'clock in a rather cloudy, though moonlit, night. The flashes were blinding and the detonations were ear-splittingly close.

After that I figured that the bombardment was all over as far as we were concerned, so I got out of the ditch and started to climb back into the bus. But just about that time, back came the bomber, this time laying another line of bombs down the near side of the field. I dived back into the ditch so violently that I lost two replaceable lower front teeth, and couldn't find them again, although I returned the next day with a searching party and covered that part of the ditch thoroughly. The near end of this line of bombs passed within about a hundred yards of the bus. I must have been pretty rattled by this time, because I remember saying aloud, "They can't do this to us," as distinctly as my remaining chattering teeth would permit. Then it occurred to me that, after all, there was a war going on and that no one but myself was responsible for my being there. Anyway, when the plane came back and laid a third line of bombs down the middle of the field I had gained enough night bombardment experience to still be in the very bottom of the deepest part of that ditch. We waited for about fifteen minutes after this last bombardment and then climbed into the bus and went to the little town of Azuqueca, where we saw our new quarters for the first time.

Our quarters there, where I spent a great deal of my time while on the Madrid front, were the most comfortably arranged quarters that I occupied anywhere in Spain. They were in a huge octagonal building and consisted of large rooms, each of which had windows on the outside of the building and opened into the large central room which we used as a dining room. The ceiling of this central room was the top of the building—with a skylight at least ten feet square. The kitchen was just off this room, so that we always had our meals piping hot. There were eight large bedrooms on the ground floor, and they were easily able to accommodate all of us pilots. The upper rooms took care of the kitchen staff and the young ladies who kept the place cleaned up, washed our clothes, and otherwise saw to it that we had all the comforts of home. This building was known locally as the *casa de pilotos* (house of the pilots) after we moved into it. There was also another big building where the mechanics were to live. On this particular night, though, due to the bombardment and the aforementioned argument, there were pilots and mechanics mixed up in both houses.

This bombardment was good proof that the enemy had an excellent espionage system. Our planes were the first ones to use that particular field, and we had landed there only about an hour before sundown. Yet on that very night the field was bombed. It was also good proof that we had been doing a considerable amount of damage, as otherwise they wouldn't have tried to get us on our first night there. In doing this they made it clear that they had obtained their information by espionage and not by the use of observation planes.

When we went out early the next morning we discovered the advantages of scattering our planes around the field. If they had been along the sides of the field we would have lost at least half of them. As it was, we lost only one plane, and that one—by some strange quirk of fate—turned out to be Chang's, which he had just brought out of the Albacete repair shops the day before. It had been boxed by three of those small demolition bombs—and they had really demolished it. There was not a single vital part of the plane which hadn't been wrecked. Even the thermometer out on the right wing-tip strut had been ruined. Poor old Chang was heartbroken.

It rained just enough that morning to keep us on the ground for a couple of hours after daylight. Later that day we made two bombardment flights—this time to bomb enemy railroad stations. On the first trip we merely bombed and did no machine-gunning. When we returned from this mission LaCalle decided that the field at Campo X was too muddy to risk landing, so we went over to the field at Guadalajara. There we loaded up with bombs and went back across the lines to bomb another station. This time we found an enemy troop train stopped at the station so, after bombing both station and train, we returned and machine-gunned the terrorised troops who were pouring out of the train. As we were dashing back into our own territory our American patrol was neatly boxed by four anti-aircraft bursts, but our luck still held. We suffered no more than a few holes in our wing and fuselage coverings.

When we got back to the field I discovered that the American guardian angel had done an especially good job of looking after me. When we were diving down doing our machine-gunning I had felt an unusual vibration start up and, for some reason or other, had decided that my upper machine guns were the cause of it. I therefore used only my two lower guns for the rest of the strafing job. When I investigated at the field, I found that my upper right gun had got out of synchronization and put seven bullet holes in one of my propeller blades and nine in the other. If I had fired that gun a few more times I would have lost a propeller blade; then the motor would have shaken itself off the plane, and I would probably have been too low to use my parachute. After cursing the armorer thoroughly in Spanish, French and English, I went over to tell Jim and Whitey how lucky I had been.

That night we had to stay in the local hotel again, so all of our luggage was hauled back from Azuqueca and placed in our old quarters. We didn't mind it, though, as we were pretty well accustomed to moving around by this time. It gave us a good chance to practise up our Spanish with the girls we had met in the *refugio*. However, with my two missing front teeth, I was having pretty tough sledding with both the Spanish and the *señoritas*. Aside from the damage done to my already questionable good looks, they caused me to lisp in a peculiar way which convulsed everyone who heard me trying to speak Spanish.

The next morning my mechanic managed to finish the job of replacing my shot-up propeller in time for me to join a bombing expedition we were called upon to make. But my new propeller was out of line and caused the plane to vibrate so badly that it shook off all four of my bombs in some farmer's wheat field shortly after we took off. I was, of course, forced to return to the field and give the mechanics a good lecture—in bad Spanish—on the subject of propeller blade alignment. They seemed to take it to heart too and went to work with a will; yet when we took off on a patrol flight that afternoon, the vibration was even worse than before. The plane couldn't even keep up in formation without any bombs, so I was again forced to turn back to the field.

Just after I landed, our emergency signal—two red flares—arched up into the air and all the Russian monoplanes took off, heading in the same direction our squadron had taken. When they returned I found that they had run into an enemy patrol and had had quite a time of it before the monoplanes arrived on the scene. None of them were injured, although several of the planes had bullet holes in their fabric.

The most important thing, though, was that the *Escuadrilla de LaCalle* had scored its first aerial victory. Ben Lieder had got behind a Heinkel (German fighter) and fired at him until he finally went down with his motor afire. LaCalle was beaming from one ear to the other when they landed. He must have been a little disappointed, in secret, because he hadn't shot down the squadron's first plane, but he didn't show it in the least. He never put in claims for official recognition of his aerial victories, anyway, although we knew that he had already shot down at least eleven enemy planes. The Russian monoplanes had also knocked down four other Heinkels, so that night the two squadrons held a joint celebration which lasted until we were ordered to bed by LaCalle.

The next day we were ordered back to our own field over at Campo X, but as my propeller wasn't ready I had to wait until just before sunset before I could go over. Then, on the way over, I discovered that the vibration was still with me. By this time I was getting a little exasperated about the whole propeller business, so that when I landed at the field I was not in a very good humor. I taxied violently up to the ramp and reported the plane's condition to LaCalle, and he ordered me to taxi over to the parking place assigned to our patrol. This place was on the other side of the field, and there were several large ponds of water on the way there. I was so furious by this time that I didn't care much what happened, so when I came to one of the largest of these ponds I decided to try to go through it instead of going around it; but its bottom was of very soft mud, so I got just about half-way across when the plane bogged down completely—in a least a foot and a half of water and mud—leaving me sitting up in the cockpit feeling as foolish as I have ever felt.

I knew I was in for it when I looked across the field and saw LaCalle racing in my direction—in too much of a hurry even to wait for his car and chauffeur. He was in a rage. "Trejo," he yelled, "you damned fool, why didn't you go around that *laguna*?"

I immediately decided that this was one time when it would be best for me not to understand too much Spanish. But by this time the American patrol boys had come over to see what was wrong, and LaCalle put Chang into service as interpreter and had him repeat his previous question. This cornered me, so I decided to try a little stalling. "Why, I thought this was as good a place to taxi as going round. What's wrong with that?"

"What's wrong with that? You idiot, what kind of damn flying training did you have in the United States?"

Then came inspiration. "I was trained at the Navy flying school and, as you can see, I am merely a trifle absent-minded."

And the plane, sitting out in the middle of that pond looked so much like a seaplane that the implication struck all the bystanders—even Chang—simultaneously. The chorus of guffaws and leg-slappings which rose immediately made any further disciplinary conversation impossible, so LaCalle stalked off, leaving us to get the plane out of the pond as best we could.

The next day the mechanics wrangled over my ship all day. They finally decided that something was wrong with the motor and checked it over completely, resetting all valve clearances and putting in an entire new set of spark plugs. During the process I test-hopped the plane twice, but there was no change in the vibration. The next morning I decided to take charge of the situation myself. I had noticed that whenever the mechanics changed the blades of my propeller they only removed the outer part of the hub. So I suggested that perhaps there might be dirt between the inner part of the hub and the propeller shaft, and that if there was, it might be the cause of the excessive vibration. They looked a little skeptical, but as they couldn't think of anything else to do, off came the propeller, hub and all, this time. Sure enough, there was sufficient grit in one of the shaft slots to throw a steam engine flywheel off balance. After they had cleaned everything off with gasoline and replaced the propeller, I gave the plane a test flight. It was as smooth as a sewing machine!

An incident cropped up, in connection with the removal of the propeller, which gives a good idea of some of the troubles we were faced with over there. My mechanic, Chamorro, was a Communist; Jim's and Chang's mechanics were Anarchists, and Whitey Dahl's was a Socialist. They got into a violent political argument that morning which ended with the declaration by the irate Anarchists that in future they were not going to help each other or the other two mechanics. Whereupon the Socialist, not to be outdone, declared that if that was the case he would not help anyone except himself, either. I helped my mechanic with the propeller for a while, but as it was a job for at least three men we didn't make very much progress. Finally I went into a huddle with Jim and Whitey and we cooked up a scheme which we thought might work.

We walked over to my plane and started looking it over and discussing it—in English, of course. Finally, we got into an argument, which grew louder and more vehement as it went along. As this was very unusual, the mechanics drew in closer to see what was up. When the argument reached the red-faced shouting stage, each of us sneered at the other two and stomped off in a different direction, cursing each other fluently in Spanish as we went. The mechanics, of course, immediately asked Chang what was wrong. Chang very gravely explained that one of us was a Democrat, one a Republican and the other an Independent. He further explained that we had got into an argument over our political differences and had sworn that in future we would not help each other, either in the air or on the ground.

The mechanics were horrified. What if one of us got an enemy plane on his tail and the other two refused to help him? What if we never again flew the beautiful formations they were so proud of? It was inconceivable! They immediately went into a very earnest conference and then spent about twenty minutes persuading us to make peace with each other. We finally gave in, but before doing so we pointed out that we could hardly be of much use to each other in the air if our mechanics failed—on account of political squabbles—to keep our planes in flying conditions.

Then the dawn broke. They saw the moral of our fake argument and went to work on my plane at once. Very sheepishly, at first, to be sure, but they soon had it in condition for the check-flight which turned out so successfully. Chang told us that he even heard one of the Anarchists say to the other, "How in hell can you expect foreign volunteers to work together in Spain if we Spaniards fail to do so?" Anyway, after that incident we never did have any more trouble as far as the upkeep of our planes was concerned.

About the middle of the afternoon our two red emergency rockets went soaring up, so off we went. On this particular day there were two layers of clouds. There was an upper stratum at an altitude of about 13,000 feet, and a lower one of large fleecy balls of white cumulus, at an altitude of about 4800 feet. As we neared the Jarama River, south of Madrid, LaCalle started leading us up and down through the clouds, so that he could take looks at what was happening both above and below them. All at once we came around a large cloud and there, about a quarter of a mile straight ahead of us, were six tri-motored Junkers bombing planes. They were in perfect formation and, having seen us, were turning away towards their own territory. Each of them looked about as big as a box car, and six of them in perfect formation made an impressive sight. LaCalle immediately put us into a right echelon of V's and then into a right echelon of echelons. Then, to our amazement, he turned left and went into a dive! We were thunderstruck. LaCalle failing to attack enemy planes! It was unthinkable.

But his maneuvers soon explained themselves. As we followed him around the left turn and into the dive, our eyes almost popped out of our heads. For there, heading right for us, were six more Junkers. These, on account of their proximity, looked even larger and more impressive than the first six. So each of us— eleven in all—went down the chute, one after the other, holding down all four machine-gun trips throughout the dive. When each of us got as close to the Junkers as he could without crashing into them, he would execute a half-roll and dive away from them. As I

58

pulled out at the bottom of my first dive I looked back and saw the leading Junkers slowly turning over—and as he turned a little further I saw the reason why. The pilot's cockpit was an inferno of flames. It turned over completely and then plummeted to the ground, bombs and all, where it crashed with a terrific explosion. The remaining planes started a left turn, still in perfect formation, although their leader had been shot down, and tried to beat us back to their own territory. With our superior speed we were able, however, to get around in front of them and get in position for another dive.

Once more we went down, one after the other, with all guns chattering away. This time one of the remaining Junkers of the leader's patrol started down in a long shallow dive with a streamer of black smoke trailing out from its center motor and with the propeller of its right motor just barely idling. He did his best to glide as far as his own territory and almost made it—he landed right in the middle of the Jarama River, with his troops on one bank and ours on the other.

By the time we finished our second dive the remaining Junkers were too far back in their territory for us to go after them, so LaCalle re-formed our planes in squadron formation and we started back for our own territory. We passed back over our second victim just in time to see our artillery start working on it. Of the first Junker we could see only a huge smoking crate in the middle of an olive orchard. I suppose the orchard owner was cursing us heartily for not shooting down our planes in somebody else's field.

When we got back home we found that the Russian monoplanes had also managed to shoot down a couple of Heinkel fighters. It seemed that the Junkers had had an escort of about sixty Heinkels—just beneath the upper strata of clouds— but after our monoplanes shot two of them on their way down the remainder decided to stay up. They had a mountain back in their territory which they eased over to and got behind. That was why we weren't bothered while we were busy shooting down our two Junkers. LaCalle was greatly pleased with the outcome of the fight and was showered with phone calls from bigwigs all over Loyalist territory congratulating him on the work of the only all-

Spanish fighting-plane squadron. He certainly deserved the credit, too, because he had got us into perfect position for our attacking dives on the unfortunate Junkers.

That night there was another protracted oral battle between LaCalle and the mechanics about their having to live in one building while the pilots lived in another. LaCalle's reasons, of course, were purely military, as he merely wanted to be able to get all the pilots or all the mechanics whenever they were needed, without having to scour the whole town for them. But the mechanics couldn't see this point. The squabble took place in the main dining room of our house at Azuqueca, and it was extremely noisy, as anyone who has heard a Spanish argument can attest. And all this time we Americans were trying to sleep in the next room. Finally, getting tired of the uproar, we came out to see what the trouble was. The mechanics of our patrol immediately told us their grievance in Spanish so fervently rapid that Chang had to act as interpreter. He asked us our opinion on the subject.

That put it squarely up to us, so we held a short meeting in our room—mostly to impress them with the amount of interest we were taking in the affair—and then issued a joint statement. Our opinion was that we considered it best for the pilots to sleep in one house and the mechanics in another, pointing out that if there happened to be an emergency night conference for the pilots it would be necessary to wake everyone up to find out who the pilots were. The reference to the possibility of losing sleep settled the matter. Our mechanics explained things to the other mechanics; they decided that LaCalle was right, after all, and we Americans were able to go to sleep. LaCalle was so pleased with our settlement of the trouble that he came around and slipped each of us an extra packet of American cigarettes.

Speaking of cigarettes, I might mention that we seldom had any trouble getting them. A package was usually issued every night to each pilot. These were always either American or Russian cigarettes. The Russian cigarettes consisted of a long cardboard cylinder with about an inch of tobacco at the end of it. They were too mild to suit us, but they were much better than the local Spanish product. We always did our best to get American cigarettes when they were being passed out.

17th February was a rather dull day. Just after the noon meal we went out on a routine squadron patrol along the Jarama front and saw two squadrons of new Italian fighting-planes—Fiats—across the river, but they wouldn't fight. When we went over after them they dived for their mountain and went home. This was rather interesting news to our general staff; they were the first Fiats that had been seen on that front for several months. Fiats were being used down South, but Heinkels usually covered the territory around Madrid.

Later that afternoon my mechanic made a few minor adjustments on my plane, so I took it up and gave it a fifteen-minute test hop. He seemed to have done an excellent job of tuning up the rigging, because the plane would almost fly itself.

Our international quarrels over the pilots' house radio culminated that night in a complete victory for us American pilots. We had a fine, large, short-wave set, and all would have been well but for the fact that the Spanish boys wanted Spanish stations, the Russians wanted Russian stations and we, of course, wanted English or American stations. The situation had been greatly aggravated by the fact that radio etiquette over there was still in its elementary stages and no one had the slightest compunction about switching off a station that he didn't like and searching for one that he did like. We four Americans and Chang had a pretty good scheme figured out at first. We would rush in—get to the radio first—and then form our chairs in a circle around the front of the instrument, effectually blocking out any would-be turners-off and searchers.

As soon as the Spanish boys caught on, they used the trick to their own advantage. And as they greatly outnumbered us, there was nothing we could do about it until this inspired night. We managed to get our hands on one of those rubber suction windshield stickers and mounted it on the end of an old billiard cue. By using this instrument we could easily reach over the human blockade and manipulate the control buttons of the radio. And the Spanish lads thought that this was so funny that they wouldn't even turn off any station that we selected by this method.

The ones who got the raw deal as far as the radio was concerned were the two Russians attached to our squadron. One was the Squadron's chief armorer and the other was supposed to be a Spanish-Russian interpreter. The armorer was called Mikael and the interpreter Elias. Since there were only two of them they couldn't very well form a blockade around the radio and we never would lend them our dialing instrument.

The interpreter, Elias, could also understand and speak a little English and was very well posted on world politics. It was on this latter account that we Americans got in bad with him right at the start. We were talking to him one night and he jokingly asked us if it was true that Huey Long was President of the United States. We solemnly assured him that Huey had been assassinated about a year before and then, a little later on, we asked him, with innocent looks on our faces, if it was true that Trotsky was dictator of Russia. Talk about an explosion! We thought that he and Mikael were both going to rush us. They had the most shocked and horrified expressions on their faces that we had ever seen. I don't think Elias ever did forgive us for that, but Mikael seemed to get over it. In fact, he and I later became fairly good friends.

The eighteenth of February was a red-letter day in the history of the *Escuadrilla de LaCalle*. About the middle of the morning our alarm rockets went up. Off we went! As usual, we were the first squadron in the air and, on this occasion, arrived at the front about ten minutes ahead of any other squadron. All at once LaCalle started waggling his wings violently (our danger signal in the air) so we closed in and got into a tight formation. Then he threw the squadron into right echelon and went into a tight Lufberry circle to the left, each plane following the other in a horizontal circle. This is a last-ditch defensive maneuver, and we looked around for the cause of it. Upon looking upward we saw that there was plenty of cause: up there, about 6500 feet above us, was a veritable cloud of Heinkels. Some of them were already on their way down and others were getting in position to start their dives. We found out later that there were about eight-five of them. Thus, with the odds about 8 to 1 against us, we began our first big dogfight.

LaCalle had warned us, long before, that if we were ever greatly outnumbered he would use this maneuver. He had also stressed the importance of staying in formation, *no matter what happened*, until he brought us out of it. On this occasion we were to see for ourselves exactly how important it was.

The first group of Heinkels to come down saw that we were in good defensive formation. They therefore fired a few long-distance rounds at us and then veered off and dived below us— where they began to fly around lazily. Ben Lieder was the first one to fall for the bait. He started down after one of the easy-looking targets. Before he got halfway down to them, three Heinkels were on his tail. We saw his plane give a sort of jerk as the three Heinkels flashed past. Then he started wavering away toward our territory in a shallow dive. When he neared the ground he tried to land in a small field, but overshot. He turned and tried again. Again he overshot, but desperately tried to land anyway. We saw his plane crash into the side of a small hill with a terrific impact. American fighting-plane pilots had given their first life in Spain.

In the meantime Jim and Whitey had also fallen for the bait. Jim luckily got down behind his man and shot him down before three Heinkels flashed by him. His plane also gave a jerk; then it came up and over in a perfect Immelmann and started back toward our territory, with his plane apparently still under control. Whitey was just getting ready to do a bit of shooting, when he noticed the inevitable three Heinkels flashing past. Then he became aware of the fact that his plane was not answering the controls. When he looked back he saw the reason why—the entire tail of his plane had been shot off. He bailed out immediately. We saw the white parachute mushroom out, but at the time we didn't know who it was.

While all this was happening I had my first good look at enemy fighting-planes. Just after getting into the Lufberry circle I looked up, and there was a plane headed right for me. I was so interested in keeping position in the formation that I merely glanced at it and noted that it made a rather pretty sight with the sun showing through a haze behind it. Then I glanced back again and noticed that there were little flashes coming through his propeller blades. It was then I realized he was shooting at me. I swung around into a sharp left diving bank, came out behind and under him and, after firing a few seconds, swung back into the formation. The same thing happened two or three more times while we were in that Lufberry circle.

About that time another squadron of our biplanes showed up and got into our formation with us. It was a Russian squadron whose commander was known as José. They were all experienced pilots and we had all learned our lesson, so we stayed in that formation for about fifteen more minutes—until the monoplanes made their appearance on the scene. It seemed that they had missed the area of the battle and gone far into enemy territory. On their way back they saw us and immediately recognized the predicament we were in. They went up and engaged the Heinkels still remaining above; while José and his men stayed where they were to intercept any who tried to come down on us.

From that time on everything went our way. Within fifteen minutes we were in undisputed possession of that area. We had shot down at least seven Heinkels and had also seen two more of our own planes go down. After flying around for a while longer we returned to our respective bases.

Our homecoming was sad enough in itself. LaCalle's patrol returned minus one plane, the Amercian patrol returned minus two planes, while the third patrol returned intact. The missing pilots were, of course, Ben, Jim and Whitey. I was the only American to return from that flight, and my return was due more to good luck than to good handiwork. When Chang and I landed and taxied in to the part of the field occupied by the American patrol, I realized for the first time just how our mechanics felt about us Americans. Jim's mechanic, Barca, and Whitey's mechanic, Juanas, evidently saw by the looks on our faces that something out of the ordinary had happened. Juanas, the Socialist, was actually in tears, while Barca, the hitherto rough and ready Anarchist, had a look on his face that I never want to see again. The Spanish people are a very emotional race and his expression was the most poignant proof of it that I have ever seen. A woman's anguish is easy to understand, but to see a huge, broken-nosed ruffian trying, unsuccessfully, to control his emotions was almost as bad as seeing Jim, Ben and Whitey getting shot down. I told Chang to try to cheer them up by telling them that the missing men might have gone back with the Russians, but I could see that they didn't believe either of us. Every time a stray plane's motor was heard, they would brighten up. Then, as it died away in the distance, they would relapse into a state of grief even worse than before.

Finally, LaCalle sent out a summons for all pilots to report to his car, which he had discreetly parked in the middle of the field so that no ears other than those on the heads of pilots could hear what transpired. He had also had a case of beer brought out and never mentioned a thing relating to the subject of aerial warfare until each of us had downed at least a couple of bottles. Then he proceeded to demonstrate just why he had been selected to lead the first all-Spanish fighter squadron to appear at the front.

"Comrades, today our squadron lost three planes," he began. "It was entirely unnecessary. The pilots disregarded the instructions and warnings which had been given to them. You had all been told that the Lufberry formation is the best defense in such a situation. And more, you had been warned that the Heinkels could dive 50 per cent fast than our ships, and you were reminded to think of other planes of the enemy besides the plane at which you were firing. The pilots who are missing forgot all three of these warnings. They left the formation, they knew there were Heinkels above, and they had eyes only for the plane at which they were firing."

Thus, without mentioning any names, LaCalle succeeded in showing us very clearly what had happened. After that he gave us a short lecture on the tactics of modern aerial warfare and wound up with a fight talk on the glory of dying for the cause. Then he had each of us down a third bottle of beer and sent us back to our planes.

But Chang and I still had to face the four mechanics of the Amercian patrol. Our own two mechanics were obviously so overjoyed at our safe return and so solicitous for our personal comfort that it was downright embarrassing, especially when the other two mechanics were feeling so badly. Barca, who usually carried a sub-machine gun around with him as religiously as a nun carries her crucifix, had even allowed it to lie neglected in the back of one of our starter trucks.

The noon meal also was embarrassing. The squadron had had only four American pilots to start with, and now I was the only one left. The Spanish pilots went out of their way to try to help me forget that sad fact. They would probably have succeeded, too, for they are a jolly sort, but for the fact that most of their well-meaning remarks had to be translated by Chang—who was almost as grief-stricken as were Jim's and Whitey's mechanics. When the meal finally ended, there was still no news from the front, so we went out to our respective patrols and brooded around under our plane wings.

Our brooding was rather abruptly ended when our two red alarm flares went floating up from the field house. We took off as usual, circling the field once, then forming on LaCalle's patrol, and streaking away for the front. I was leading the decimated American patrol and Chang, who usually lagged behind a bit, was flying very close formation on my plane. We arrived at the Jarama River just in time to see three Junkers coming toward us from the direction of Getafe, an enemy field south of Madrid. They had the usual escort of Heinkels over their tails, but this time our monoplanes were up above to take care of them. The three Junkers saw us a long way off and immediately started turning. We gave our planes full gun and fired at them all the way back to their mountain, which was just barely showing above the lower layer of clouds. This was far within their territory, so we turned back across the lines.

Then began one of the strangest games imaginable. LaCalle would dive for the ground, as though we were returning to our field. As soon as we got down near the ground he would lead us up a valley until we were well out of sight of the front lines. Then we would go across country until we came to another valley and sneak back up to the river. There we would open up our throttles and dash up through the clouds, bursting through them like a flock of mad goats, trying to catch the Junkers sneaking back for another try at our lines. Twice we performed that maneuver, and twice we caught them in the act. But each time they sighted us in time to get back to the safety of their mountain. But that time our gas was so low that we had to return to our home field.

That was our last flight of the day. Back at the field we learned that in the morning's combat four of our planes and seven of the enemy's had crashed on the field of battle. But at 5:30 we were told that an American pilot had landed at Alcalá de Henares, one of our other fields, badly wounded in the leg. Which American, we couldn't find out. Then, at the evening meal, a telephone call came through. It was answered by one of the Spanish pilots, but he couldn't understand a word that was being said, so Chang was called to the phone. After listening for a moment he let out a loud whoop and shouted, "Whitey!"—so we at least knew that Whitey was still alive. The joy of the Spanish pilots was evident on their faces.

Whitey had had his plane's tail shot off but had landed safely about a mile back of our front lines. He expected to be with us again the following day. At that time he was speaking from a little town right on the banks of the Jarama River. About that time the phone rang again and we were further elated to hear that Jim had been the pilot who landed at Alcalá. He had been struck in the calf of his right leg and had lost a lot of blood, but he was in no immediate danger and was resting easily. But we still had no news of Ben. We didn't find out until the next day that he had been killed in that crash landing he had made after being shot.

As soon as we heard this last news LaCalle commandeered a huge bus and everybody—pilots, mechanics, armorers, chauffeurs and all—set out for Alcalá to see Jim. When we arrived there we were told that he had been sent to the *Hospital de Sangre* in Madrid. But when we arrived in Madrid—my first visit there—we found that he was not at the *Hospital de Sangre*, so we went back to Azuqueca and turned in for the night. That hospital in Madrid—it was located in the old Palace Hotel—had certainly been very appropriately named when they called it the "hospital of blood," for there was blood all over the place. They had evidently had a very busy time of it that day.

CHAPTER VI

AFTER WHITEY BAILED OUT

The following day we had a fairly easy time of it out at the field. During the noon meal we learned that Jim was in the military hospital at Alcalá and had been there ever since having been treated in the emergency clinic at the flying field. We immediately made arrangements to visit him that night. After sunset three carloads of us dashed over to Alcalá and finally located Jim in a little room in the military hospital. He was looking very well and told us that he expected to be back on the line in about twenty days. We left him some cigarettes and a couple of bottles of cognac and went back home, where we found Whitey waiting for us. While we were eating dinner he told Chang and me all that had happened to him. Chang translated it into Spanish for the benefit of the other boys.

"Just after we went into that Lufberry circle I saw a Heinkel down below, merely fiddling around, flying slow and making banks from one side to the other—and before I knew what I was doing I had my plane diving down after him. I had him all lined up in my sight and was just starting to shoot when—out of the corner of my eye—I saw a greenish shadow flash past on my right. I realized then the danger I was in and pulled back on the stick with the intention of climbing back up to the formation again. But the plane would not come out of the dive. I swiveled my head around and my eyes almost popped out of my head when I saw where my tail assembly had been. There was nothing there but a few strips of fabric trailing out behind. Then I found I couldn't get either one of the cockpit doors open. The plane had gone into a funny kind of skidding spin and I suppose some sort of strain had been set up that clamped the doors shut. And that plane was making knots toward the ground by that time. Somehow or other—I don't know how myself—I managed to squeeze out.

"I had another scare, though, when my right foot got stuck in the opening. Believe me, I did some foot-shaking. That plane

68

finally came off like a rubber boot does when you kick it off. I don't remember pulling the rip cord, but I suppose I did, because the chute opened and almost cut me in two when my weight hit it. I was about 1500 feet up when it opened, and when I saw that I was on our side of the river I started singing and shouting—some sort of reaction, I suppose. But I soon knocked that off, because about that time a couple of those low-flying Heinkels came over and started shooting at me. Fortunately, before they could make more than a couple of passes, a patrol of our monoplanes came whistling down and chased them off. I finally landed near a country road in some fellow's olive grove.

"After I landed, several farmers and soldiers came up, and when they heard the way I spoke Spanish they immediately assumed that I was a German pilot, and I thought they were going to shoot me on the spot. They contented themselves, however, with merely taking my pistol away from me and starting me off down the road under guard. Before we had gone very far we met another group of soldiers, and one of them knew just enough English to understand that I was an American flying for the Government. By way of verification I showed him several papers I happened to have from the Air Ministry. After that they apologized all over the place. They returned my pistol and even borrowed a donkey from one of the local farmers and helped me climb aboard. The worst thing was that everyone I met insisted on giving me a drink of the exceptionally foul-tasting wine they carried in those little leather gadgets. Anyway, I finally arrived at a little town just across the river from San Martín de la Vega, which the Fascists have.

"I was taken to the commander of the Loyalist garrison there, and I almost fell over when I saw that it was commanded by a woman—a Captain Dolores Something-or-Other. Whoever she was, she certainly had her men well in hand. They really snapped to when she spoke. She had a phone call put through to Madrid and they got me a straight-through connection to here when I arrived there last night. I couldn't get away then on account of a shortage of transportation, but I didn't mind that at all.

"She took me to one of the lookout posts and let me take a look at the Fascists walking around over in San Martín. They seemed to be within rifle range, so I asked her why they didn't crack down on them. She gave me the astounding reply that they never fired upon each other during the *siesta* period. They certainly have a system!

"That's about all there was to it. A few hours later I got word that a car from Madrid was waiting for me in front of garrison headquarters, and in a couple of hours I was in Madrid. Then this morning I was sent to Alcalá, where I gave the group commander a statement about the affair. I hung around the flying field over there all afternoon, and they finally managed to spare a car for me to make the trip over here. Nothing to it." He yawned, and then added, "Oh, yes, I forgot to mention that Captain Dolores traded pistols with me before I left the garrison. She wanted something to remember me by. Don't tell my wife about it, though."

Nothing to it! Just a matter of getting shot down, shot at in a parachute, almost getting shot by our own men, meeting an Amazonian garrison commander, and seeing an air battle from the ground. The way he told it we almost wished that we could go through something like that ourselves. At any rate, he didn't have any trouble holding the attention of his audience; we were all sitting around with our mouths hanging open during most of the narrative. By the time he finished telling the story it was almost midnight, so we were all hustled off to bed by LaCalle. We were all divided between elation at Whitey's safe return and depression at the sign of the empty beds of Jim and Ben.

The next day, the twentieth, we had the honor of giving the starting signal for the Government's counter-attack on the Jarama front. For eight or ten days the Rebels had been concentrating on that front. Their object was to cut the road connecting Madrid and Valencia, and they had eventually succeeded in pushing a salient across the river which was threatening to accomplish just that. By the twentieth, however, the Government had brought in sufficient reinforcements to feel that a counter-attack could be started. Everything was planned to begin at 1:30 p.m. during the *siesta* period. We were to start the ball rolling by bombing and machine-gunning artillery emplacements in the salient.

LaCalle got us into perfect position at just the right time, and down we went. Our own troops had laid out large white triangles on the ground just back of their first-line trenches, so there was no danger of making any mistakes—for some had been made before this scheme was worked out. We spotted two new emplacements, well back in the salient, which the Fascists had not had time to camouflage, and made them our bomb targets. By this time we were fairly expert bombers, so we managed to sprinkle bombs all over the two unfortunate emplacements. Then we flattened out our dive a bit and machine-gunned the enemy infantry from the rear, catching them—as had been planned— either eating their midday meal or indulging in their after-dinner *siestas*. Immediately after us came José's squadron, which machine-gunned whatever we had happened to overlook. At the same time our artillery cut loose and our infantry went over the top. All this time two of our monoplane squadrons were upstairs to see that no enemy planes came down on us from above.

As soon as we finished our machine-gunning we flattened out our dive a bit more and headed for home. We had a rather narrow escape back of our own line. One of our own anti-aircraft batteries—which evidently hadn't got the news—fired one salvo at us at point-blank range before recognizing our red-striped wings and fuselages. However, the damage done was to the metal streamlining shield on one of LaCalle's wheels. The wheel itself was fortunately not damaged at all. When we landed at Campo X, though, one of the pilots, Ortiz, in Berthial's No. 3 patrol, hit a soft spot and his plane nosed over. It was another of those slow nose-overs, so Ortiz wasn't even scratched.

On this flight LaCalle had reorganized our American Patrol— naming Whitey Dahl as leader with Chang and me flying the wing positions. Whitey did a very creditable job, as our patrol's bombardment was very good. The effectiveness of our entire organization's teamwork was proved by the information we received later that our troops had driven the Fascists back to the river and had captured their artillery emplacements complete with large supplies of ammunition. Both the guns and ammunition turned out to be of German manufacture.

Shortly after our return from this flight the familiar red flares went up and we did likewise—streaking to the front behind LaCalle. He didn't even circle the field this time, but only slowed up long enough for the stragglers to catch up with us and then kept his throttle wide open all the way to the Jarama. From these unusual proceedings we knew that something important was up. And sure enough, there were our three Junkers friends of the day before—with their usual escort of fifty or sixty Heinkels up above. Again our monoplanes were up there to take care of the Heinkels, so LaCalle threw us into left echelon and we went in—one after the other—to attack the Junkers. Again they managed to turn so that all of their machine guns could bear on us, forcing us to fly through a veritable hail of bullets. I was in so close to Whitey that I was almost firing in formation with him. We each fired for about thirty seconds—until we were about a hundred yards from the Junkers—and then went into our half-rolls and dove away; noting, as we did so, that one of them was dropping out of the formation. As we pulled up and around into formation again, though, we could see one of our own biplanes headed for the ground in a crazy and obviously out-of-control flat spin. Even as we watched, it crashed into the ground.

By the time we regained our altitude two of the Junkers had made it back to their mountain and the third had glided across the river and made a crash landing behind its own lines. It crashed well in sight of our ground observers, however, so the squadron got credit for it. We then climbed up to where the monoplanes were heckling the Heinkels and took a hand in the festivities. And those Heinkels were certainly on the spot. They could out-dive our biplanes, but they knew they couldn't out-dive our monoplanes. On the other hand, they could outclimb the monoplanes at high altitude, but they couldn't outclimb our biplanes. When they saw our two squadrons of biplanes coming up they started edging over toward their mountain, and when they thought they were close enough the whole swarm of them dove for it together. About five of them, though, failed to make the grade. Two of them burned in the air and the other three crashed into the mountain they were expecting to protect them.

We cruised around for a while after the last Heinkel left the scene of action, and then wended our weary way home. When Chang finally re-joined Whitey and me in patrol formation we at least had the satisfaction of knowing that it wasn't his plane the Junkers had shot down.

After all planes had landed, we learned that one of the planes of the third patrol was missing. We had no way of knowing which one it was until LaCalle called us in for the usual conference. Then we found that we had lost one of our ablest and best-liked Spanish pilots—Berthial—leader of the third patrol. He had also been the second in command of the squadron after LaCalle. His loss left us with only eight out of the original twelve members of the squadron, Calderón, Ben Lieder and Berthial having been killed, and Jim Allison being so badly wounded as to be out of active service for the time being. We found out later that Berthial had been struck in the forehead by two steel-jacketed bullets— which speaks well for the marksmanship of some German machine-gunner.

Our effectiveness that day was attested to by the bombardment which the Junkers treated us to that night. They bombed all over the Henares River valley from 9:30 p.m. until after midnight. We had a rather good time of it, though, in the local bomb shelter in Azuqueca. As we had to be out at the field all day, we had no opportunity to see the town girls except in the bomb shelter during these bombardments. This bomb shelter was also an old wine cellar. It had a new side passage, but it otherwise it was the same as it had been for the last two or three centuries. A short description of our activities during the bombardment on this particular night might help to give an idea of what goes on in a small civilian town with a relatively small number of combatant guests.

At about 9:30 we received a phone call warning us that enemy bombers had been heard crossing the front lines. At that point the ladies of the household and all the civilians of the town were warned and betook themselves to the three wine-cellar *refugios* of which the town boasted. At the time we were engaged in drinking Málaga wine and listening to Chang with a ukulele and a Spanish pilot with a guitar harmonizing on various Spanish tunes. Shortly thereafter we heard the outlying sentries' rifles being discharged, and our house guard came in to warn us that the Junkers' motors could be heard in the distance. We went into our respective rooms, put on our coats, and went out into the street. There we could hear the motors ourselves—also dull detonations off in the direction of Guadalajara—so we turned to the right and walked about fifty yards to the corner house on the other side of the street. Turning left around its corner brought us to the entrance of the wine-cellar bomb shelter or *refugio*. There we stopped to look up at the starry sky and listen to the drone of the Junkers' American-made Wasp engines. Occasionally the darkness off in the distance would be relieved by lightning-like flashes, and a few seconds later we would hear the dull thudding detonations of exploding bombs. At this time the nights were bitterly cold, so we soon made our way down into the cellar.

Its entrance was a very old arched doorway. A stone stairway led down to a landing about ten steps below—from which a four- or five-step stairway turned to the right and led to the floor of the cellar proper. It was about forty feet long, twenty feet wide, and ten feet high. The new passage had been sapped out of the left side and was approximately twenty feet long and ten wide, with seats down its sides and a lighted candle at its end. It was filled with the older people of our part of the town. Two or three older women were evidently terror-stricken, but the remainder were making a gossip-fest out of the affair. The floor of the cellar proper was crowded with the younger people and the members of our squadron.

Whitey, Chang—who still had his uke—and I started singing the only American tune that Chang knew, *Yes, Sir, That's My Baby*, and soon we had ten or twelve of the best-looking *señoritas* around us. It goes without saying that we made the most of the occasion. The young ladies took no end of joy out of teaching us the latest popular Spanish tunes while Chang played the accompaniment on his uke. We were all sitting on the edge of a large stone trough, and after one of the songs we heard a plaintive cry behind us. Investigation disclosed that the owner of the cellar had placed a nanny goat with twin kids on a bed of straw in the trough. We almost got into trouble with our new-found girl friends on account of the amount of attention we gave to the twins—not even Chang had seen twin kids before. However, during the following song fest, in which we taught the girls American tunes and they taught us Spanish ones, all was forgiven. Chang and I had the best of the situation, for Whitey was still a bridegroom at heart and was very seriously being true to his wife. My missing teeth gave Chang a slight advantage over me, but that was compensated for by the fact that I could make dates with two or three of the girls at a time and then, if any misunderstandings occurred later, could use my ignorance of the language as an excuse. Around midnight we decided that the bombardment was over, so all went home and turned in.

The next day wound up our work of helping our infantry push the Rebels back across the river—and they didn't seem to need very much help at that. In the morning we had an emergency call and dashed up to the Jarama front, but weren't able to locate anything that looked like an enemy plane. We sat around the rest of the day gambling, but just before sunset LaCalle came dashing up in his little car and told us to get ready to take off at once. We were to protect José's squadron while it bombed and machine-gunned a few Fascists who were still on our side of the river. This was another of our very effectively timed attacks. Until this time it had been unheard of for front line troops to be bombed within an hour or so before sunset. On this occasion José's squadron bombed them after the sun had actually set. After he finished his work and got away safely we went down and used up most of our bullets—some 5000 apiece—and came back home just in time to land before absolute darkness set in.

When we landed we heard that our infantry had worked in perfect coordination with us and that this side of the Jarama was completely ours. We also heard that, the night before, the city of Albacete had received one of the worst night bombardments of the war. It had lasted about five hours and over 400 civilians had been killed and about 2500 wounded. Fifteen soldiers who were there on furlough also were killed.

The following day we sat around the field all day but had no action. The Fascists had evidently give up any idea of trying to get across the Jarama again. Whitey and I collected four *duros*—

75

five-peseta pieces—and started our old game of coin pitching again. Much interest was taken in it by the mechanics and other personnel of our patrol. They all tried their hands at it but couldn't seem to get the knack of making the coins land on edge and stick. They showed us how to play one of their own coin games which could be played at much less expense—10 céntimos per game—but we were just as clumsy at it as they were at our game. When another dull day followed, Whitey and I tried to teach Chang our coin game, but he was so unbelievably clumsy at it that we wouldn't even gamble with him. As I have mentioned before, he was a sergeant in the regular Spanish Air Force and his salary was about 800 pesetas a month. On the other hand Whitey and I, being contract men, were drawing down a salary of about 18,000 pesetas a month. We naturally felt that we should not do any gambling with him under those circumstances, especially in view of the fact that all the Spanish boys, including Chang, were under the impression that we were only drawing second lieutenant's pay—about 1500 pesetas a month. We finally settled on a system of playing with Chang for one peseta per game, letting him win every now and then.

From the twenty-fourth of February to the fifth of March we had very bad weather—either rain or a zero ceiling—so we had a good chance to study the ex-count's estate. Our landing field must have been used to pasture his horse, because it was as smooth as a billiard table and there wasn't a sign of the usual levees and embankments that were to be seen in that neighbourhood in other fields. The field proper was a square of about three quarters of a mile to the side. At its southern end an additional square, of about a quarter of a mile to the side, had been added. As the wind was usually from the north, we always had plenty of room for our landings. The field house was over in the northeast corner, in a small grove of trees, on the banks of the overflow valley of the Henares river.

About two hundred yards up the bank was the walled estate. At the right of the large, arched, carriage-capacity gateway to the patio was the residence of the count. It was a long two-story building, on the lower floor of which were the two dining rooms I have mentioned. The end of the building nearest the gate had evidently been built before the rest, as it was considerably higher and the stones were more weather-beaten. This higher portion was square and was decorated at each corner with Moslem minarets. There was a sort of storage attic in this portion which proved to be a veritable treasure trove for Whitey and me, who were not averse to a little looting on the side. By delving into the débris I managed to accumulate an old dueling sword—which was taken away from me at the border some months later—two or three rather aged paintings, an assortment of spurs, and a leather shepherd's pouch, which I have so far been unable to find a use for. Whitey's selections were made with about the same degree of intelligence.

The sewing room on the second floor was a favorite hangout for Chang and me. It was presided over by Cristina and María, two sisters of twenty and twenty-two years, respectively. They were city girls, having been evacuated from Madrid some months before, and were very well educated in comparison with the other girls who worked around the building; these had only learned to read and write since the beginning of the revolution. Cristina had completed high school and María had attended the University of Madrid for two years. They had been assigned to the sewing room because they were the only ones who understood the operation of the new American sewing machine with which it was equipped. María was a typical Spanish brunette, but Cristina had very light-colored brown hair. Contrary to the general belief, there are quite a few light-haired people around Madrid. Cristina was slightly the better-looking, although María was still far above the average in the United States.

There was always gaiety in the sewing room. Anyone hearing the two girls singing happily over their work would never suspect that their home in Madrid had been destroyed and that they had a father and two brothers fighting in the trenches defending the city, or that a third brother had already given his life for the cause. But, as I have said, the Spanish people had seen so much death and destruction that they had become accustomed to it.

Cristina was Chang's favorite, while María was generally conceded by the other pilots to be my *novia* (sweetheart). As a matter of fact, we did get along exceedingly well. Much of my acquisition of the Spanish language was accomplished under María's tutorship in that cheery room. Before she took a hand in my education I had been struggling along with an English-Spanish grammar and a small dictionary and hadn't been making much progress.

During these bad-weather days Chang and I would wait until the girls' working day was over and then the four of us would go back to town together. Usually we walked, leaving Whitey, the dutiful spouse, to go back in the car with the chauffeur. Occasionally, however, we took the car for spins along the Madrid-Guadalajara highway, leaving Whitey and the chauffeur to walk the mile or so to Azuqueca in each other's company. What they thought of that arrangement we could only guess, although their rather sour facial expressions assisted us a bit in our guessing. We usually got back to the pilots' house barely in time for dinner at 8:30.

Our evening meals during these days of idleness were always gay affairs. They were served in delightfully casual courses with long enough intervals between them for the entertainment provided by arguments and jokes—which Chang translated both ways. Here we had an opportunity to observe the gestures which seem to be such a necessary adjunct to the Spanish language. LaCalle was especially violent when engrossed in an argument or telling a story.

At one of those evening meals, LaCalle was at the head of the table and I was sitting on his left. He was relating some anecdote or other and still had his knife in his left hand, so that I was in imminent danger of losing an ear. Finally, when his hand stopped momentarily right in front of my face, I reached out and removed the knife from it, laid it on the table, and resumed my meal. No one at the table—except Whitey and me—moved for at least ten seconds; even Chang was frozen with astonishment. LaCalle was so surprised that he couldn't even lower his hand from the position where it was when I took the knife. He was looking first at the knife, then at his outstretched hand, then at me. Finally, Whitey let out a huge guffaw, and in an instant the whole table joined in. LaCalle struggled with his military dignity for a few seconds and then he, too, joined in the laughter. After that we were never bothered with flying cutlery in front of our faces.

The Russians from Alcalá came over to have dinner one night. They told us that they had an American pilot in their squadron and, upon being questioned further, said that he was blond and that they called him Alberto. Albert Baumler, who had been with us at Manises! He had been sent to the training school at Los Alcázares in time to go through it with Koch, and they had been assigned to a Russian squadron which was working down on the Málaga front. Then they had been transferred to this squadron at Alcalá.

On the twenty-fifth, Whitey, Chang and I went in to Madrid on our first recreational visit. On way we stopped off at Alcalá to see Jim, who seemed to be getting along all right and told us that he was going to be sent to Valencia in a day or so. Arriving in Madrid after dark, we couldn't see very much of the results of the bombings and shellings, but we could see that the Madrileños were prepared for anything. There were stone barricades across the principal streets, with an opening on each side barely large enough for a car to squeeze through. Each barricade had a group of guards assigned to it, and they inspected every car that went through.

After we passed the last of the barricades and got into the center of the city it looked just like a city in normal times. Everything was wide open; the street cars were running as usual; theaters were operating, and night clubs were enjoying an unusual boom. We helped out the boom by visiting all that we saw on the way to our destination, which was the Florida Hotel. Champagne was hard to get, but we managed to pick up a bottle here and a bottle there until by the time we got to the hotel we were pretty well loaded, both inside and out. Whitey agreed to carry the champagne while I arranged for rooms with bath; we had already decided that we were each going to stay in the bathtub so long that we would need two of them. As there were five bottles, he had quite a time with them and almost got into trouble at the elevator while I was having the contents of our passports transferred to the hotel registry.

Whitey had managed to get the elevator down (it was one of those automatic affairs), but after he got inside he couldn't reach the control buttons to make it go up again. He was also unable to reopen the door to get out. After about two minutes of this a huge fellow with a mustache came along and wanted to go up on the elevator, too, but as he saw Whitey was already inside he waited awhile, expecting him to go either up or down. When Whitey failed to do either, the large stranger opened the door and asked him, in Spanish, what the hell he thought he was doing. Whitey, not understanding him, asked in English why in hell he hadn't opened the door instead of standing there with his mouth full of teeth. Whereupon the stranger, in perfectly good American, answered that people shouldn't get into strange elevators unless they were sure they could get out of them. Whitey almost fell on his face when he heard himself answered in English, but soon recovered and explained his predicament and had the stranger do his button-pushing for him. I saw the last part of this act and asked the man at the desk who the stranger was. He proved to be no other than Ernest Hemingway, the famous writer.

We had two rooms up on the seventh floor, and just outside of Whitey's room was a huge hole in the corridor floor. The lady in charge explained that it was only a shell hole, and showed us where the shell had entered the building through the wall at the end of the corridor. After that we indulged in the first hot baths we had had since leaving Valencia. I think that was the most luxurious feeling I have ever had—getting into a modern bathroom after a month or so of icy bathing in makeshift accommodations. We lay in the tubs for about an hour before getting dressed and going down to the tea room, where we bribed one of the waiters to bring us champagne glasses and a bucket of ice. After polishing off a couple of the bottles of champagne we climbed into our car and motored back to Azuqueca, feeling that it wasn't such a bad war after all.

A day or so later, however, we disgraced ourselves. We asked LaCalle for permission to go to Madrid again, and he gave it to us on condition that we be back in the house by 11 p.m. This time we arrived at the Florida Hotel quite a bit earlier than we had before, and in the lobby we met several American writers, including

Herbert Matthews of New York Times, Gorrell of the United Press, and Whitey's friend of the elevator incident, Ernest Hemingway. This meeting, of course, called for a few rounds of Scotch and soda. When this ended we went up to indulge in hot baths. This time Chang was along with us, so we had engaged three rooms for the occasion. We couldn't get them on the same floor, so we made arrangements to meet in the tea room afterwards. Whitey and I finished at different times, and each was afraid that the other might forget to get the champagne. As a result, when we finally met at about 9 o'clock, we each had a couple of bottles under our arms. This gave us a formidable obstacle to overcome. At 1:30 we had finished only three of the four bottles, but we decided that we had better start for home. Within a few minutes we embarked in our car—opening the other bottle en route—assuring ourselves that we could easily sneak in without LaCalle being aware of it. The next morning, however, when we were out on the field, LaCalle came around and asked each of us in turn the time of our arrival the night before. I was the first of the culprits to be questioned. As I was feeling extremely guilty and extremely bad, I hid behind my supposed ignorance of the Spanish language and couldn't understand a word he said. Whitey, strangely enough, was also unable to understand anything. So LaCalle called over culprit number three—Chang—to act as interpreter. Being thus cornered, I ventured the supposition that we *might* have been in by midnight. Whitey, being next, approached honesty a bit closer by supposing that it *might* even have been as late as one o'clock. Chang indicated his English tutoring by averring that his watch had stopped so he really couldn't say, but he thought that Whitey and I *might* be right. LaCalle indicated his belief in our respective stories by informing us that we were all under arrest for a week—during which we would not be allowed to leave the vicinity of the field or the town except when we had to fly. Feeling rather downhearted, Chang and I went over to be comforted by Cristina and María, leaving pour old Whitey to comfort himself as best he could.

On March second I endeavored to put one over on LaCalle and ended up on the wrong end of the deal. He came around one day and I declared that I had a formidable toothache—*un dolor de diente formidable*. When he questioned me I made matters worse by asserting that, in fact, I had two teeth aching formidably. I even went so far as to show him the two teeth which were supposed to be aching, pointing out a couple of molars in my lower left jaw. He looked rather thoughtful and then said the Spanish equivalent of "very well" and drove off. A little later he came back with the chief of the airdrome and had me show him the two teeth. He then loaded the chief and me into a car and sent us in to Madrid to a dentist he knew. The chief went in and talked to the dentist first, and then I was called in. The dentist turned out to be a huge fellow, and after getting into the chair I discovered to my horror that he couldn't understand a word of my newly acquired Spanish. Before I could get clear, he pulled both of the molars I had claimed were aching and looked a little disappointed because there weren't any more of them "aching".

On the way back to the field the chief told me that I was to go back to the dentist's office in about two weeks so that he could take plaster casts and start work on a lower plate for me. As I have mentioned before, I lost my two replaceable lower front teeth during that first bombardment of the field. So my little trick didn't turn out so badly after all. It would at least result in my being relieved of the embarrassment of going around with a couple of front teeth missing—and at a cost of only two molars!

Our first replacement pilot made his appearance March third. He was a tall dark-haired fellow named Velasco and had a rather wild look in his eyes. There were no extra planes available at the time, so he immediately got himself in bad by trying to crawl into this or that plane parked around the field. As each plane already had a pilot, he only succeeded in getting himself kicked out of every plane on the field. Pilots hate to have anyone except themselves and their mechanics fool around their planes. We finally saw him examining the wreckage of Ben's, Whitey's and Berthial's planes, which had been hauled in from the front and left near the field house. He seemed to be thinking of building his own plane. "That fellow came up here to fight," Whitey remarked.

Chang informed us that the newcomer had been in the Air Force before the war but had been confined in a hospital for mental observation. Naturally we felt no end cheered up by this information. If all our replacements turned out to be of this stripe, there would be no telling what was likely to happen up in the air. Happily, all the replacements sent up later turned out to be excellent men.

All this time we were being treated to bombing raids practically every night but, since Chang and I had ingratiated ourselves into the good graces of the two best-looking girls in town, we didn't mind them at all. Whitey, still faithful, finally refused to go to the bomb shelter. It was too cold, he said. As soon as we shoved off for the *refugio* he would turn in. One night, though, the Junkers tried to bomb our local railroad station and missed. The bombs—four 225-pound bombs—landed about 200 yards from the pilots' house, breaking every window in the building. Whitey kicked up gravel on both turns sprinting for the *refugio*—arriving there clad in nothing more than his underwear—when his fright immediately turned into embarrassment. He then had the nerve to try and borrow one of the two or three coats with which Chang and I and our two girl friends were each equipped. We jeered at him for a while before relenting and sending one of the house girls—women know their place in Spain—to the house to get Whitey's cold-weather flying suit. After Whitey bundled up in that he was fairly comfortable and left Chang and me to our own devices—or vices.

We went back into action again on March sixth and found that the Fascists had a new type of bomber. Our field was still too wet to land on, but we could take off from it. Our two red rockets soared up between a couple of rain squalls, so off we went, splashing mud all over our spotlessly clean planes. We arrived at the front just in time to intercept two bombers headed toward Chinchón, one of our base towns back of the Jarama front. They were above us when we first saw them and endeavored to make their objective, but it was just a little too far. They saw us divide and start climbing so they too divided, each turning away from the other in a 180 degree turn. As the nearest one passed over us we saw that it was one of the fast, new bi-motored Junkers which we had been hearing about lately. We fired a few rounds at them, but as they were approximately as fast as we were they managed to get away.

They certainly were sleek-looking things and were obviously piloted by experts. When they separated, after a false start by the slightly nervous left plane, they executed the turn beautifully. After making their turns they came together again in perfect, though inverted, formation. When we returned to Campo X, LaCalle decided that it was too muddy to land on, so we went over to the grassy field at Guadalajara and landed. We had to wait quite a while before our cars and starter trucks came over from Campo X. It began to rain heavily shortly after we landed, and we had a cold nine miles' drive back to Azuqueca that night.

We had an equally cold drive going back to the Guadalajara field the next morning. At about 9:30, while we were all eating breakfast, an enemy observation plane came out of the clouds directly over the field. What a scramble! We dashed out and jumped into cars and trucks and sped across the muddy field to our planes. The first patrol of monoplanes, however, were the only ones ordered to take off. As the ceiling was very low, the enemy plane went up into the clouds and easily eluded them. It was a Heinkel 71, known among the Spanish pilots as a *Paloma Blanca* (white dove) on account of its being painted white. These planes are very fast mono-motored jobs carrying one pilot and one observer and had been doing most of the enemy's observation work up to that time.

CHAPTER VII

THE ITALIAN DEBACLE

On March eighth we received two more replacement pilots—Lecha and Blanche. They were each given about an hour in which to practise take-offs and landings so that they could get used to the rather rough landing field. Also to give LaCalle a chance to see what kind of pilots they were. Blanche turned out to be an exceptionally good pilot. Lecha was only fair, having had very little previous flying time.

That night Chang told us a very interesting story about Blanche. He had been over in Spanish Morocco when the rebellion broke out, had pretended to be a Fascist sympathizer, and was assigned to the job of co-piloting a large seaplane bomber, the chief pilot being a Spanish Rebel captain. One of the plane's two mechanics was also a Loyalist sympathizer, so the two of them got together and did a little secret plotting. At the first favorable opportunity, Blanche gave the signal by shooting the chief pilot dead and taking over the controls himself. While he was doing this, his consort was busy shooting up the other mechanic and the rear machine gunner. Whereupon Blanche set a course for Loyalist territory and landed the plane in the harbor at Valencia, where he was received with wild acclaim. The grateful Government immediately made him a first lieutenant in the Loyalist Air Force, and he flew seaplanes for a while until he decided to try his hand at fighter planes. The Government immediately granted his request and sent him to Los Alcázares for training. When he completed the course there he was sent to the Escuadrilla de La Calle, and we were certainly glad to have him.

At that particular time LaCalle was having a bit of trouble finding someone to lead the third patrol, which Berthial had been leading. He wanted to give me the job, but I fell back on my ignorance of the Spanish language as an excuse for staying with Whitey and Chang. When he saw the way in which Blanche handled his plane, he immediately made him the third patrol leader. All hands concurred in the opinion that they had made a very wise choice.

On this day we also received word that the enemy had started a drive on the front to the north of us—the Guadalajara front. The attack was started from the Fascist-held town of Sigüenza, which is forty-odd miles north-east of Guadalajara. It consisted of three columns, highly mechanized, advancing down the main highway connecting Madrid and Zaragoza. It was, as we found out later, the beginning of the famous Italian offensive on the Guadalajara front. At any rate, they managed to advance several miles before nightfall that day. The Government troops put up a strong resistance with machine guns and light field pieces, but they were gradually forced back by Mussolini's tanks.

March ninth was a rather eventful day. Early in the morning our alarm flares started us off, and hardly had the last plane cleared the ground when we saw three bi-motored Junkers coming out of a low-lying layer of clouds which began just north of the field and extended northward as far as the eye could see. They also saw us climbing up and the sight so rattled them that they dropped their bombs in the river and fled. We managed to get in a few long-distance shots at them, but they were too fast for us to overtake.

Shortly after that a *Paloma Blanca* came over—presumably to see how much damage had been done. We took off again and gave chase, but it took to the clouds as usual and we never caught a glimpse of the thing again. On this occasion there was quite a muddle up in the air among our planes. Only two patrols took off—the first patrol and our American patrol. LaCalle was caught by surprise over in the field house, so Chato Castenedo led the first patrol. He was flying in LaCalle's plane, and we naturally supposed that LaCalle was in it. The plane's peculiar maneuvers, however, caused us to wonder whether LaCalle was going a little soft in the head. Finally the whole outfit went through a big cloud, and when we came out of it there wasn't a sign of the first patrol. When we looked around, though, we discovered that they were all flying in formation on our patrol. When we landed we discovered the cause of the confusion. Chato explained that he had decided that he didn't know enough about squadron landing to handle the situation. He had therefore decided to put the burden on Whitey's shoulders.

The Italian troops made considerable headway that day. Early in the morning they captured three small towns near the main highway—Almadrones, Argecilla, and Ledanca, and continued their advance. All this time it was raining heavily, which was to our advantage. Their central column was pushing down the main highway sweeping all opposition before it. Our soldiers lacked the equipment for combatting tanks and armored cars; but after about a third of the column had crossed a bridge near an important crossroad, the bridge was washed out by the flood due to the unusually heavy rains. This kept the majority of this most important column out of action for several hours during the most critical part of the advance while the bridge was being repaired. The vanguard of the central column continued its advance for three or four miles, but it was not strong enough to consolidate its newly-captured positions and was forced to retreat. The washing-out of this bridge was a great blow to the Italians, since it frustrated the entire advantage of their mechanized army—speed and surprise.

In the meantime the Italians to the east of the main highway had also been making considerable progress. They surrounded the town of Brihuega and captured it shortly before nightfall. They had advanced so rapidly that they were within the city limits before the Government commander was even aware that they were in the vicinity. As Brihuega is only about fifteen miles from Guadalajara, there were some awfully long faces around our dining table that night. And our spirits weren't at all uplifted by the two- or three-hour bombardment we were treated to that night. That was the only occasion I can remember when there was no singing or laughing in a bomb shelter during a bombardment. Even the usually cheerful Cristina and María were looking a little sad and thoughtful that night.

The following morning was dismal and rainy, with clouds almost down to the valley floor. However, the ceiling lifted for a while, so LaCalle sent Whitey out on a reconnaissance flight over the Italian territory. When he returned he reported that many troops were moving on enemy roads back of the lines. We immediately loaded up with bombs and got all set to take off. Just about that time, though, the ceiling dropped back to zero again and stayed there the rest of the day. All we could do was sit there grinding our teeth and listening to the heavy artillery booming away in the distance. LaCalle would come around every now and then and give us the latest news from the front.

The news on this day wasn't as disheartening as that of the day before. Our high command had taken advantage of the enemy's delay, caused by the bridge washout, to send up reinforcements as fast as they could get them there. Among these reinforcements were the eleventh and twelfth brigades of the International column, which were sent up during the night. They immediately entrenched themselves in the valleys and *arroyos* which extended westward from Brihuega. Our espionage system also discovered that Italian headquarters had been moved up to the little town of Trijueque, located on the main highway due west of Brihuega. It rained so heavily and continuously on this day that neither side was able to do very much fighting.

Whitey, Chang and I went into Madrid that night and almost got bombed on our way back at the little town of Torrejón de Ardoz. The Junkers were trying to bomb the railroad station there, but instead they hit the area about halfway between the station and the highway, which were about two hundred yards apart. We just barely had time to jump into the ditch before the bombs started falling. We stayed there for about half an hour before continuing on our way to Azuqueca, where we were bawled out by LaCalle for being twenty minutes late; but we had the shrapnel-slashed top of our car to back up our story, so we were exonerated.

The eleventh of March was another wet day, with occasional heavy clouds coming along scraping the ground. About the middle of the morning we loaded up with bombs, nevertheless, and took off between rain squalls for our first look at the Guadalajara front. We cruised along over the very low clouds, with only an occasional glimpse of the ground below, and fortunately found an opening just over the place we were supposed to bomb, so down we went. We dropped our bombs at an altitude of about 600 feet and then went the rest of the way down with all four machine guns hammering away. The Italian troops were certainly in a bad way down there. The continual rains had made a regular quagmire out of that entire section of the country, and they were practically without protection from our aerial attack. What trenches they had been able to dig filled up with water almost as soon as they were dug. They didn't seem to have any anti-aircraft guns at all at that time, although a few of their field guns opened up an ineffective fire on us. We could see the poor devils scurrying through the mud in all directions as we came down spraying them with bullets. We made only one pass at them, as we had instructions to hurry back to the field before the ceiling fell to zero again.

That afternoon we learned that there was very little fighting going on at the front. The adverse weather conditions kept the Italians from using their machinery, so they were practically stalled. Their trucks, armored cars and even their tanks were forced to stay on the main highways. Our side was taking advantage of the situation to rush in reinforcements and armament. The Government had managed to get in some modern, rapid fire, large-caliber guns enabling our men to play havoc with the enemy's stalled motor units. These guns would have done much damage but for the fact that the men were unaccustomed to their operation.

About two hours before sundown we loaded up with bombs and took off again. This proved to be a tactical error; hardly had we left the ground when the clouds converged and we found ourselves right in the middle of a terrific thunder, lightning and hail storm. LaCalle gave the landing signal and went over to the river and dropped his bombs—we had orders never to land with bombs, as several pilots had been killed that way—the rest of us doing likewise. By that time there were planes all over the sky—flying through the rain, hail, and lightning flashes. Our patrol stayed in formation until Chang pulled his head down in his cockpit so that he could reach his bomb release. He then slid over and almost rammed my plane, missing it by about six feet. This rattled him so much that he sheered off into the rain and never did find Whitey and me again.

LaCalle landed safely, but the rest of them were having difficulties; two or three of them were trying to land at the same time and nearly had collisions. Whitey and I watched this performance for a while, the storm getting worse all the time, and then decided to head for Albacete while we still had a chance. Neither one of us had a map, but somehow or other we managed to get there. We landed about an hour later, wondering how many of our squadron mates had got down safely.

As soon as we identified ourselves we were taken to the pilots' house, which was about two miles from the field. There we met the Russian Commander-in-Chief, General Douglas, and several of our Russian friends whom we had met at Alcalá. They located a Russo-English interpreter and when they heard our story called up Alcalá immediately to tell them that the two Americans were safe. They also told them to pass the word along to LaCalle at Azuqueca. After that we were led down to a very sumptuous dining room. The place had formerly been a duke's hunting lodge and was furnished and decorated like a palace. After an excellent meal we sat around talking to the American wife—Mrs. Rose-Marie—of an American pilot who was flying transport planes for the Government. She could also speak Russian, so our Russian friends were able to join in the conversation. After a couple of hours of this we were shown to our quarters and turned in for the night.

Early the next morning we went out to the field and discovered that we were to fly back to Alcalá with no less a personage than General Douglas himself. We naturally assumed that we would be assigned the job of flying protection over some slow-moving transport plane. Our eyes almost popped out of our heads when we saw the general come out and climb into a fighting-plane just like the ones we were flying ourselves. We had heard of generals in the United States flying—but they merely flew long enough to qualify for the 50 per cent extra pay to be derived thereby. But here was a general actually flying himself up to the front in a single-seater fighting-plane!

Anyway, we took off with the general in V formation and were over Alcalá about an hour later. When he gave the break-up signal we sheered off, as previously instructed, and headed for

Guadalajara. When we landed there, it was just as though two prodigal sons had returned. Our two mechanics, Chamorro and Juanas, were overjoyed to see us. They had given us up for lost when we failed to return the day before, and had only halfway believed LaCalle when he told them that we were safe in Albacete. They even had brand-new packages of American cigarettes ready for us; and American cigarettes were rather scarce at that time.

When we went in to make our report to LaCalle we received a half-hearted calling-down for leaving the vicinity of the field so soon. However, we could see that he was pleased to see us back safely. In fact, Chang later informed us that he had heard LaCalle bragging to the Russians about how two of his pilots had been able to find the field at Albacete in such adverse weather conditions without a map. We also found out that the rest of the boys had climbed up above the clouds and flown around until the squall passed. Then they had all come down and landed safely, with the exception of Chang, who had got himself lost and finally tried to land in some farmer's newly-ploughed field. Naturally, his plane had nosed over. He was not hurt in the crash, however, and had been retrieved shortly before midnight.

The squadron had already made one flight across the lines that morning and we had arrived just in time for the second one. On this flight we had a double mission to fulfil. We were to protect a squadron of our heavy bombers while they bombed and then, when they finished, go down and do our dive-bombing and machine-gunning; or, in other words, mop up after them. We climbed to 8000 feet directly over our field and waited until the heavy bombers came along. They were flying at about 3200 feet, so we came down to 6500 feet and accompanied them across the lines. Even from that height we could see that a great battle was in progress down below. The flashes of field artillery from both sides were almost continuous. The appearance of our aerial fleet turned out to be the beginning of the end as far as the already-retreating Italians were concerned.

Three of our heavy bombers made a direct hit on and around the crossroad north-west of Brihuega and completely ruined it. They also wrecked fifteen or twenty trucks and cars which were trying to retreat and had become involved in a traffic jam there. A huge truck, whirling end over end through the air, made a most impressive sight. As soon as our bombers were safely back in our territory we dove down on the poor devils ourselves and cut loose with both bombs and machine guns. After that we went up to about 1000 feet and started cruising around.

This crossroad was the only avenue of retreat for the motorized units of the central and part of the eastern Italian columns. The fields were so muddy that they were forced to stay on the two roads leading from this crossroad to Brihuega and Trijueque. Even the foot soldiers had trouble retreating through the mud which, being very sticky, accumulated in large lumps on their feet.

As no enemy planes appeared, we had nothing at all to do except watch the progress of the battle below and help to demoralize the Italians. Immediately after the aerial bombardment, our tanks (Russian) started to advance slowly through the mire, followed by cavalry, which proved to be worth its weight in gold in this engagement. By that time the Italians were so demoralized that it was almost terrible to behold. Rifles and ammunition belts were abandoned to facilitate running and away they went. That misery loves company was illustrated by the way the fleeing wretches tended to group together as they ran. This was very bad judgment indeed, because at the first sign of a group of men, down would come one of our fighting-planes with all four guns chattering away. That was part of the instructions we had received before leaving the field. A description of one of these murderous dives will give you an idea of what the foot soldiers may expect in the war to come.

I spotted one especially large group of Italians in wild retreat before a couple of tanks. My first move was to maneuver my plane to a downwind position from them and then push its nose over into a sixty-degree dive. At that altitude—1000 feet—the men looked like a mass of ants on the ground, even through my telescopic sight. At about 700 feet I opened fire with one upper and one lower machine gun. This was so that I could see, by the tracer bullets, whether or not I was on target. The stream of bullets was just ahead of the fleeing group, so I opened up with the other two guns and pulled the plane's nose up a little.

By this time I could see individuals plainly; they had also become aware of my presence. Then they did the worst thing they could have done—started running in the opposite direction. I could see dead-white faces swivel around and, at the sight of the plane, terror would turn them even whiter. Some of them tried to run at right angles, but it was too late; already they were falling like grain before a reaper. I pushed the rudder back and forth gently, so that the bullets would cover a wide area, then pulled back on the stick—just as gently—thus lengthening the swath. I pulled out of the dive about twenty feet off the ground, zoomed up to rejoin the squadron, and started looking for more Italians. We kept this up until our gasoline and bullets were so low that we were forced to return to the field.

Late in the afternoon the weather cleared up enough for us to make another trip across the lines. Once more we loaded up with bombs and climbed above the lower layer of clouds. Just as we got into position for bombing, we spotted a squadron of Italian fighting-planes—Fiats—headed in our direction. LaCalle failed to see these and went right on about his bombing. We thought he was merely ignoring them, so we followed him down and did our bombing and machine-gunning. When we got back to the field we found that both our patrol and the third patrol had been fired on—one plane in each patrol coming back full of holes.

Chang's plane was the one shot up in our patrol—it had thirty-five or forty bullet holes in it. He had been, as usual, lagging back out of position in the formation. The funny thing about it was that he thought someone in the third patrol had been shooting at him; he had not seen the Fiats at all. In fact, he didn't even know that he had been under fire until he landed and his mechanic pointed out that his plane was full of holes. Then he immediately wanted to go over and fight everyone in the third patrol. It took all of Whitey's eloquence and mine to convince him that he had actually been under fire from enemy planes.

That night we received very good news from the front lines. Our troops had advanced as far as the crossroad and were busy consolidating their positions. They had captured a large number of enemy cars and trucks which had been unable to get past the bombed crossroad. The territory the Italians still held on the west of the main highway was so mountainous that the use of anything on wheels was out of the question. We had inflicted an enormous amount of damage on the enemy that morning. Our heavy bombers had destroyed several columns of trucks on the highways and our own bombardment and machine gunnery had entirely broken the morale of the Italian first-line troops.

The same bad weather was in evidence the next day. In the morning LaCalle sent Whitey and me across the lines on a reconnaissance flight to check up on the movements of the enemy. We spotted several convoys of trucks and two or three long freight trains between Jadraque and Sigüenza. We also discovered that they now had anti-aircraft guns, as we were fired at several times. All of this we marked down on our maps so there would be no chance of forgetting anything. On our way back to the field we saw three bombers off in the distance headed toward enemy territory. Whether they were ours or theirs we never did find out. We had had strict instructions from LaCalle to do nothing except reconnoiter and protect ourselves.

That afternoon we loaded up with bombs and, just as we were getting ready to take off, our two red flares went floating up. Fortunately, we were all sitting in our planes with our motors idling, so we all went off at once—except two or three who habitually lagged behind. Just as Whitey and I came around in our first turn we saw three bi-motored Junkers come out from behind the clouds overhead. They saw us at once and their gunners immediately opened fire, although they were a good 4800 feet above us. The pilot of the Junkers on the right was evidently a bit nervous, because he deserted the formation and started for his own territory full blast. I have often wondered what happened to him when he reached his camp. The other two held course and speed and tried to carry out their mission. They were trying to hit the railroad station but they overshot, and their bombs landed right in the middle of the old Hispano-Suiza buildings at the end of the field—just as the above-mentioned laggards were taking off over that area.

Although we were weighed down with bombs, Whitey and I started climbing at once, and were soon up to the level of the two remaining planes; but as soon as we got up to their level they dived into the thick clouds and started for home. We finally saw one of them streaking through the clouds below and went after it—opening fire as soon as we lined up our sights on it. Its rear machine gunner also opened fire on us: we could see his tracer bullets coming our way. However, we hit either him or his gun, because after about ten seconds of firing his stream of tracer bullets ended abruptly. We fired at that plane until it scrambled back to safety in the next cloud. Then we went back to rejoin the formation.

The rest of the squadron had all tried to close in with the single plane which had left the formation, but it had too great a start. Blanche, the new leader of the third patrol, managed to fire at it a few seconds before one of its gunners shot the tail off his plane. He immediately bailed out and pulled his parachute rip cord. Then we were horrified to see the parachute string out above him and fail to open. The entire squadron saw him strike the ground, about 6500 feet below, with terrific force. LaCalle re-formed the squadron and we went on across the lines and carried out our bombing mission—using up the rest of our bullets on the enemy troops as we were returning.

Chang had gone down to the spot where Blanche struck and had memorized the location thoroughly before returning to the field. By the time we returned he had already started out after the body in our patrol car. They returned about half an hour later. For the rest of the time during which we used that particular car we had a rather grim reminder of our ex-squadron mate in the form of a large bloodstain on the rear cushion. His parachute had failed to open because it had been wet, so they immediately started checking up on all our parachutes.

The front line reports we received that night were more cheering than ever. It seemed that our infantry had made two very effective counter-attacks. The first had been made against the town of Trijueque and had been supported by tanks and planes. The support from the air had consisted of two squadrons of bombers protected by a squadron of monoplanes. They had

95

made five trips across the lines that day and had done outstanding work. The tanks, as usual, had advanced after each bombardment. The second attack, above Brihuega, had cut the enemy lines between Brihuega and Torija. This placed the Italians occupying Brihuega in the most dangerous position.

That night Whitey, Chang and I took a run in to Madrid after the evening meal. We all met our American newspaper friends and indulged in another hot bath. When we got back home we discovered that we had missed an unusually good bombardment. Three houses on the edge of the little town had been destroyed. In fact, the more timid of the town's citizens were still in bed when we got there an hour after it happened. Before we turned in, LaCalle came around and told me that I was going to lead the third patrol whether I wanted to or not. Blanche's death that day had again left it without a leader.

CHAPTER VIII

MY FIRST AERIAL VICTORY

The next day, March fourteenth, there were heavy rain squalls, with a ceiling that ranged from zero to 1600 feet. About the middle of the morning we loaded up with bombs and started across the lines. Just after we got across we ran into a squadron of Fiats. LaCalle immediately gave the danger signal—violent waggling of the wings—and dropped his bombs. The rest of us also dropped our bombs and closed in on LaCalle's plane. As the enemy planes were to the left and higher than we were, LaCalle put the squadron in right echelon and began climbing and closing in on them.

Their leading formation, a seven-plane echelon, went into action against LaCalle's and Whitey's patrols. There was another patrol of five Fiats up above the first one, and this entered the fray about the time my patrol got there. What a scramble it turned out to be! At first the planes were so thick and travelling so fast that side shots were all I could get. Finally, though, I got behind one of the luckless Fiats and fired at him steadily for about fifteen seconds. When I pulled away from him his plane was already in its earthward spin, with gasoline, water and very black smoke trailing out behind it. That was my first positive aerial victory. It gave me so much self-confidence that it almost proved to be my undoing.

I immediately got on the tail of another Fiat, but it was much harder to hit than the other, probably because it had a more experienced pilot. I played around with him for several minutes before he finally dived away from me. Then I looked around to take stock of the situation and discovered that I was alone. The rest of my squadron was fully a mile away, getting back into formation, and there, about 2000 feet above me, were five Fiats! Their leader had already started into his dive down on my plane when I discovered them. I was certainly on the spot—alone with five enemy planes above me. I knew that if I started for the clouds 3000 feet below they could out-dive me. As time was getting short I decided to try a little trickery.

I went into a dive toward the clouds below, keeping an eye on my rear-view mirror and the first of the enemy planes framed therein. Just before he lined up on my plane I pulled around in a sharp left vertical bank. He was traveling too fast to be able to follow me, so all he could do was keep on going down. I completed a 360-degree turn —cadets at Randolph Field take notice: your training maneuvers aren't as meaningless as they may seem—and came out directly behind him. I fired steadily at him until the next plane was about to line up, and then pulled the same maneuver on him with the same results. This occurred twice more before I submerged my plane and myself in the comforting security of the clouds.

This was a good illustration of the advantage that experience gives to a fighting-plane pilot. If I had become involved in a situation like that in my first dogfight I would have headed for the clouds in one long dive, and would certainly have been shot down. As it was, I knew that I could outmaneuver the Fiats and managed to dodge four of them. Experience is still the greatest teacher.

When I came out below the clouds, however, I discovered that I was in totally unfamiliar territory which, as far as I knew, might belong to the enemy. It was very mountainous country and the ceiling was so low that most of the mountain tops were up in the clouds. As I had no map, I set the old familiar course for Albacete, 160 degrees. I had to thread my way through the valleys until I finally got out of the mountains and flew out over the rather extensive valley in the province of Albacete. I must have passed to the north of Albacete, though, because after about an hour and a half of flying I passed over another mountain range and saw the deep blue of the Mediterranean before me. I had come out a little south of Valencia and immediately recognized the familiar promontory of Cape San Antonio off to the right. Thereupon I turned left and headed north for Valencia, which I could already see in the distance.

I arrived over the field at Manises in one of the worst windstorms I have ever tried to land in. Just as I came over the field I saw one of the huge transport planes which were parked on it being blown backward, while men tried frantically to hold it in one place long enough to be staked down. Ordinarily I would have waited a while before landing, but my gas indicator was bouncing up and down on zero, so I had to land right away or take a chance of having to make a dead-stick landing in that wind. Just as my wheels touched the ground an unusually violent squall whistled across the field. In a twinkling the plane was about fifty feet in the air and in a stall. People familiar with aviation terminology will know that this comes under the heading of "Serious Situations." However, I blasted away with the throttle and my 750 horses went to work with a will. Even with that power the plane was just barely able to hold its own; but it was sufficient to ease the plane down to the ground again.

As soon as the wheels touched the ground I cut the gun again, and the wind was so severe that the plane only rolled about thirty feet before coming to a complete halt. Then I had to open the throttle about halfway and push the stick forward to keep from being blown backward. I held it there, with motor and stick, until about twenty militiamen ran out and helped me to taxi in to the shelter of the commercial hangar. There I examined the plane and found that, except for a few bullet holes in the right wing, I had come out of the battle unscathed. The mechanics who examined the plane also informed me that I had landed with a practically non-existent supply of gasoline, as I had not over five liters left in my tank.

As it was entirely too windy to think of taking off, I went into Valencia and put up at the Hotel Inglés. As soon as I got cleaned up I went down to the Vodka Café, and whom should I find there but Jim Allison and Charlie Koch! Jim's leg had developed an infection, and he was being sent back to the States. Charlie had developed stomach ulcers and was also on his way back. He had had several hemorrhages which had almost finished him off before he decided to get out of fighting-planes.

Charlie told me about the adventures he and Baumler had had before he had been forced to leave the front by stomach trouble. They had both been sent to a squadron in which all the other pilots were Russians. Charlie had managed to shoot down a Fiat

99

while on duty down at the Málaga front. We swapped stories until about midnight, and then I went back to the hotel and turned in for the night.

The next day I was up bright and early and went out to the field in the pilots' bus. After waiting around all morning another biplane fighter came in, with a Russian pilot. I then learned that the two of us were going to escort a transport up to Alcalá that afternoon. We took off later for Albacete, loaded up with gasoline there, and took off again for Alcalá. When we arrived there I left the convoy and went over to the field at Guadalajara.

The squadron was coming in from a mission across the lines, and my arrival was the cause of a rather humorous mix-up. It seemed that they had had a slight brush with enemy planes, so naturally everyone was anxious to see if all of the planes returned safely. They hadn't noticed my plane when I joined the landing circle so, when one more plane landed than had started out, everyone was puzzled. Some even thought that an enemy plane might have got mixed up and come home with them. However, the mystery was cleared up as soon as they made out the number on the side of my plane.

That night, when we got back to the pilots' house, I discovered that we had received some new replacements for our more or less depleted squadron. Among them were no other than Manuel Gómez García, who had been with us at Los Alcázares, and Barbeitos, whom we had met at Manises. They arrived just in time to find out all about our night bombardments, for that night we had one of the most vicious bombardments we had ever experienced. It lasted from 9:30 until after 11:30 p.m. First the enemy dropped heavy bombs indiscriminately all over the countryside, concentrating on the vicinity around Alcalá. Whitey, Chang and I stayed in the bomb shelter for the first hour or so and then got tired of it and turned in anyway. Every now and then we could hear a plane droning over, and they all seemed directly overhead; but nothing ever happened nearby, so we soon dropped off to sleep.

While down in the *refugio*, though, we had heard the latest news from the front, and it was certainly encouraging. The Italians were being pushed back steadily all along their lines and were suffering heavily from our aerial attacks. Captured Italians had stated that they were all completely exhausted and that, because of the heavy rains, their commissary department was unable to get provisions up to the front lines. Some of them had not eaten anything for several days. They also stated that the general in command of their division and two of their battalion commanders had been killed; both of the commanderless battalions were completely disorganised. Another curious point was that practically all of the captured men thought they had been fighting in Ethiopia. Their officers, of course, knew where they were, but a great proportion of the foot soldiers were completely deluded. Their disillusionment was made more complete by the fact that most of the prisoners had been captured by our Garibaldi Battalion, made up entirely of Italian volunteers fighting for the Government. They formed part of the International Column, along with the American Lincoln Battalion, and were credited with outstanding work during the battle of Guadalajara.

Early the next morning we received word to load up with bombs and stand by to protect a squadron of our mono-motored bombers, which we were to meet over Alcalá. We had never seen any of those planes before, so we were all a little curious as to what they looked like. We showed up over Alcalá at the appointed time and sure enough, there they were. They were huge crates, very slow, and were each carrying about a half-ton of small demolition bombs. There were about twenty-four of them, and they were so slow that we were forced to drag along at a speed very close to our stalling point—very uncomfortable. They evidently knew their business though, because in spite of a considerable amount of anti-aircraft fire, they lumbered into perfect position over the enemy lines and let go, with the result that about a mile and a half of enemy trenches went up in the air. Then, as soon as they got back to our altitude we went down and dropped our own bombs, and also threw in a little machine-gunning. As we were going down in our dive I could see our tanks charging up to attack the demoralized Italian troops all along the lines which had been bombed. The tanks put the finishing touches on the show there.

When the tanks appeared, the Italians started running down three roads which led from the attacked territory. These three road converged at a crossroad and there was a fourth road which meandered off to the north. The Italians were trying to get to this northward road, and just as the traffic jam was at its thickest six of our bi-motored bombers sailed majestically out of the clouds overhead and bombed the crossroad. Three of them bombed at a time and as far as I could see they all made either direct or near-direct hits. The slaughter was terrific; this time I saw several huge trucks spinning through the air, end over end, with men flying out of their open rear ends. As soon as the smoke settled we went back down and started machine-gunning the survivors. While we were taking care of them our tanks, supported by cavalry, came up and captured everything that had been cut off by the destruction of the crossroad. We afterward learned that they had captured over 1,000 trucks, about 100 machine guns, 25 field pieces and large quantities of ammunition.

While we were busy ground-strafing, José's squadron of biplane fighters had a brush with Fiat fighters off in the distance. One of the Fiats managed to hit the gas tank of one of our fighters, which immediately caught fire and started down. The pilot had evidently been hit too, because he went down with his plane. It flamed brilliantly as it went through the air and was an awe-inspiring sight as it gracefully curved down, finally striking the earth some 10,000 feet below with a terrific explosion. Baumler's squadron, under Kosokov, came up at about that time and gave José a hand, and they managed to shoot down two of the Fiats before the remainder of them made good their escape. Baumler got one of them. That was the last we saw of the Fiats for several days.

By that time our gasoline was getting rather low and most of us were completely out of machine gun bullets, so we were forced to return to the home field. There we heard that our ground troops had more than carried out their mission, and that our assistance would not be needed again that day except to protect them from possible enemy bombardments. It was just as well too, because about that time it settled down to a more or less steady drizzle.

Nevertheless, at about 1:30 that afternoon we saw our two red alarm flares go soaring up, so off we went, heading for the front as fast as we could. We arrived over Brihuega just in time to head off five bi-motored Junkers bombers. Seeing us at just about the same time we saw them, they turned tail, went into a slight dive and headed for home. We weren't even able to get within firing range of them. Then, a couple of hours before sunset, we had another alarm and dashed up to the front to find our five adversaries trying to sneak across the lines again. This time we chased them far back into their own territory, until we were flying through clouds of anti-aircraft bursts, before turning back. When I landed I discovered that I had received two anti-aircraft holes in my propeller—one in each blade. One was about six inches from the end of one blade and the other was about ten inches from the end of the other blade. They were both about the same size, so they almost counterbalanced each other and I was able to continue using the same blades for a while. I also had a few holes in the fabric of wings and fuselage, as did other planes in the squadron, but they were quickly patched up with airplane glue and pieces of fabric off wrecked planes.

March seventeen started out with the ceiling at zero, and it didn't lift once throughout the entire day. Under those conditions we weren't able to make any flights. In the afternoon, however, our commander-in-chief, General José Miaja, visited the field and inspected all hands. He was a jolly-looking old fellow, about sixty years of age, wearing horn-rimmed spectacles; and he earned our respect by keeping us standing at attention for as short a time as possible. He gave us a short speech, praising us highly for our work of the past few days, and then had LaCalle dismiss the formation. After that LaCalle led each of us pilots up and formally introduced us to the general. Then he showed the general how quickly our guard patrol could go into action by firing the emergency alarm signal.

It was a genuine test, too, because the boys on guard duty out on the field hadn't the slightest idea as to what was going on. Whitey and his second patrol were on duty at the time. Within twenty seconds after the alarm was fired they were all in their planes with their motors turning over. The general was so highly pleased that he had them called in to the field house at once so that he could congratulate them personally. I was sent out with my patrol to relieve them while they came in. Needless to say, when General Miaja departed he left a most profound and lasting impression upon all of us. Just before he left, he gave out the information that the Italian general in charge of the entire enemy offensive had been wounded in the fighting of the night before.

The next morning we had an emergency meeting shortly after arriving the field. We took off, got into squadron formation, and scurried up to the front just in time to intercept the same five Junkers. Again we saw the advantage of fast bombers, because once more they were able to turn and slither back into their own territory before we could get within firing range. With the extra speed they were able to pick up in their slight dive they were even able to outdistance our planes, which were in a slight climb. Their departure left us with nothing else to do but take out our spite on the luckless Italians retreating on the main road down on the ground below.

That afternoon LaCalle came around to each patrol with a large military map and an air of great secrecy. He showed us where we were to bomb and where other squadrons were to bomb, the bomb sites disclosing to Whitey and myself at once that our troops were going to close in on Brihuega in a timed attack in conjunction with our aerial attacks. We finally took off with everything we could carry and met a huge fleet of our mono-motored bombers over the flying field at Alcalá. They moped along past Brihuega and did their usual bit of very efficient bombing, after which we dived and dropped our own bombs in our assigned area. Then we clawed back up to the base of the clouds, at about 4800 feet, and started cruising around on the lookout for enemy fighters.

Shortly afterwards a squadron of our bi-motored bombers—Katiuskas—came along and bombed the daylights out of the Italian trenches again and then went home to stay. Then the Katiuskas showed up again and dropped some more heavy bombs on what was left of the Italian artillery. As soon as they were through, our tanks started advancing on the ground below, backed up by cavalry. All this work had been carried out in

104

clouds of anti-aircraft fire. They must have concentrated all their anti-aircraft guns in that district, but through the entire campaign on that front they weren't able to bring down a single plane.

As soon as our tanks started their advance, we started diving down and machine-gunning any enemy trenches which were still intact. We kept this up until scarcity of gasoline and ammunition again forced us to return to the home field. We stayed on the ground for the rest of the day, counting the captured Italian trucks which passed in a continuous stream as long as we were on the field. Our mechanics counted over 800 over them, so we knew that the official score of more than 1000 was somewhere near correct. Just before we knocked off for the day LaCalle came around with the news that our troops had recaptured Brihuega, along with a lot of new Italian equipment.

On this day I was also given two new wing men in place of the two I had had, who were atrocious formation flyers. My two new men turned out to be the best front line pilots I was ever to have in Spain. One of them, Justo García, was a native of the city of Guadalajara and knew all the surrounding countryside by heart. He was also one of the least excitable Spaniards I ever saw. The other one, Magrinán, was a trifle excitable, but an excellent formation pilot. I made the last flight of the day with them on the wings and was greatly pleased with the performance they turned in. LaCalle had also given them a talk, before sending them to my patrol, on the ability of American pilots, so that everything I told them was accepted as gospel truth.

That night Manuel Gómez, the Mexican pilot, gave us the news about the other Americans who had been at Los Alcázares with us. It seemed that Bell had been unable to pass the flight tests and had been sent back to the United States. Dickenson, while unable to pass the fighting-plane check, had been checked out as an observation pilot and was stationed up around Barcelona somewhere. Jim Allison and Charlie Koch, both ill, were on their way back to New York.

The next morning was another nasty one, with the ceiling hovering around zero most of the time, but with an occasional clear patch drifting across the field. About the middle of the morning LaCalle came around and told me that I was to make a reconnaissance flight over the Italians' territory the first time I had a chance to take off. He also said that I was to take one of my wing men along to fly protection. I chose Justo for the job, and as soon as the next clear spot came along we took off. We couldn't get past the plateau north of Guadalajara, though, because the clouds were right down on top of it, so we were forced to return and report absolute failure. We had done our best, though, both having almost crashed into a hillside while trying to fly through the murk.

We waited until afternoon and then, when an especially large clear space came along, took off for another try at it. This time we were successful and managed to get over to the Italian-held city of Cogolludo. From there we followed the railroad north-west to Sigüenza, then flew over the main highway and followed it back to Guadalajara.

The trip back along the highway was quite interesting. The clouds were only about 1600 feet off the ground, so we were forced to fly very low. I was flying at an altitude of about 300 feet, while Justo, flying protection, was at an altitude of about 1200 feet. For several miles we were under fire from both anti-aircraft guns and 50-caliber anti-aircraft machine guns. Fortunately, we were too low for the anti-aircraft guns to be effective, but the 50-caliber machine guns certainly gave us something to think about. I would see a stream of their tracer bullets off on to one side or the other and immediately dodge away from it, occasionally even dodging over or under the stream, which looked just like a stream of water from a hose.

In the meantime we could see the Italian troops in their trenches on each side of the road. They seemed to be under the impression that they were going to be bombed immediately, because they were all lying flat in the bottoms of their rather shallow trenches. It was certainly a relief, however, when we finally crossed the front lines and got back over our own territory. Our troops immediately recognized the brilliant red markings on our planes and gave us a tremendous hand as we sailed by about ten feet off the ground. It gave them a big kick to see their own planes apparently ignoring the Italian anti-aircraft as being too erratic to even bother about. They didn't know that the clouds forced us to fly so low. We could see them jumping up and down and giving us the Government military salute (clenched fist), which we returned.

At any rate, when we got back to the field we were able to report to LaCalle that the Italians seemed to be running out of the Guadalajara area as fast as they could. We had seen a couple of trains and a few convoys of trucks, but they had all been headed in a northerly direction. When LaCalle discovered that we had come back over the main highway at an altitude not exceeding 1200 feet he was extremely irate. He even went as far as to intimate that, while he didn't give a damn about our hides, fighting-planes were not only expensive but also hard to get up to the front. However, when we pointed out that we had flouted the entire Italian anti-aircraft defense system without getting a single hole in our planes, he relented a bit. In fact, Chang later told us that he hot-footed it right over to the Russian squadron and started bragging about his pilots. To make his joy more complete, while he was over there, reports came in from the front lines to the effect that two crazy Loyalist pilots had steamed down the entire Italian-held section of the main highway under a terrific volume of anti-aircraft fire and got away with it. When we arrived at the pilots' house that night he was still trying to look displeased, but wasn't succeeding at all.

LaCalle called us all in to the field house on March 20 and announced a complete reorganization of the squadron. Instead of the usual three patrols, as before, there were going to be four. He was to lead the first, as usual; Whitey was to lead the second, as usual; I was to lead the third, as usual; but Manuel Gómez was to lead the fourth—most unusual. Hardly had we finished our arrangements and gone back to our planes when the emergency alarm was fired, giving us a good chance to practise our new formation. We dashed up to the front, but this time we weren't able to sight the enemy bombers, so we practised formation flying for a while and then went back home. Gómez did a pretty good job of leading his patrol, considering that he had not had any practice at that sort of thing for several years.

That afternoon we had another timed meeting with the

Rasantes—single-motored bombers. This attack was carried out perfectly. They dropped their bombs and went home; then we dropped ours and flew back up above to fly protection while our Katiuskas came along and did their work. This was all carried out near the town of Cifuentes, about twelve miles east of Brihuega.

Late in the afternoon we tried the same stunt again, but this time ran into difficulties. Just as our Rasantes came out of the clouds over enemy territory we saw three Junkers bombers, escorted by about twenty Fiats, directly ahead of us. All of us immediately dropped our bombs and went into action. LaCalle led his patrol in against the Junkers; Whitey led his against the Fiats to the left; I led mine against the Fiats to the right; while Gómez led his men against the Fiats up above. LaCalle's attack on the Junkers forced them to drop their bombs in their own territory and head for home as fast as they could travel. Whitey's attack on the Fiats to the left sent them into the clouds, and they were not seen again that day. As I turned to the right I passed through the edge of a cloud and lost Justo, so that when I came clear on the other side I had only one wing man, Magrinán, still flying with me. However, there were only two or three Fiats off to the right, so we closed in on them. Two of them promptly dived into the clouds and left, but the other very gamely tried to outmaneuver us, with no luck at all. I got behind him and fired steadily for about thirty seconds; whereupon his plane immediately went into its final spin and crashed into the ground nearly 5000 feet below; so I checked off my second aerial victory.

While all this was going on, Gómez had led his patrol in against the upper formation of Five Fiats. After closing in with them he looked around and discovered that he had no wing men and was alone. Naturally, five Fiats made short work of one Government plane, and when we returned to the field Gómez was missing. LaCalle told us that night that he had landed in our lines badly wounded.

Later that night, at the pilots' house, we got the news concerning the results of the day's work up at the front. Our early afternoon timed attack had resulted in the destruction or capture of more Italian equipment. The Italian troops concentrated in that vicinity had also been utterly routed by our own troops; in their haste to retreat they had abandoned all their personal equipment and a number of field machine guns. During the dogfight which occurred on our last flight, five enemy planes had been shot down in our own lines by our own and another squadron before the remainder of them fled in great disorganization. While this was going on, our ground troops had continued their advance and captured the towns of Utande and Munduez. A large quantity of medical supplies was captured in one of these towns.

LaCalle also showed us some official stationary that had been captured. On the back of the envelopes, in monarchist colors, were the words, *"Viva España! Viva Franco!"* (Long Live Spain! Long Live Franco!) Then, up in the upper left corner of the envelope fronts were the colors of the Bourbon family with the words *"Una Patria, Un Estado, Un Caudillo. Una Patria— España, Un Caudillo—Franco"* (One Country, One State, One Chief. One Country—Spain. One Chief—Franco.) A rather strange combination to have on the same envelope.

The last ten days of March and the first few of April brought us so much bad weather that we spent a good deal of the time on the ground. At the field several important changes occurred. Whitey, after a severe attack of stomach pains, was sent up to Madrid for treatment. Then Chang was ordered suddenly to report to the group commander at Alcalá, leaving me the only remaining member of the original group. And most important of all, LaCalle was promoted to a major and turned over active charge of the squadron to El Capitán Jiménez. That was the end of the *Escuadrilla de LaCalle.*

Jiménez, though an excellent pilot, was far from being the natural leader of men that LaCalle had been. He was rather vacillating and did a little too much thinking for his own and the squadron's good. In other words, he was too cautious. He immediately got in bad with all pilots by decreeing that each patrol, in numerical order, should be on duty for two hours at a stretch throughout the day. Also that the pilots of the duty patrol should sit in their planes, in full flying equipment, during this two-hour period. He also reorganized the squadron into three patrols again, instead of the four which LaCalle had only recently ordained. In the new organization he was leading the first patrol; I was leading the second, with Justo, Magrinán and Chang as wing men and Ortiz was leading the third.

CHAPTER IX

A RURAL ADVENTURE

I made a rather interesting reconnaissance flight on the third of April. The weather wasn't good enough for general flying activities, but it was ideal for an observation flight in a fast fighting-plane. There were huge banks of fluffy cumulus clouds flowing along near the ground and above them was a solid layer of lead-colored nimbus clouds. Justo and I were sent out on our usual flight back of the Guadalajara front, and we were able to sneak along between the lower clouds very close to the ground. Whenever we ran into anti-aircraft fire all we had to do was dodge around in the clouds and the gunners would be completely baffled. If we saw any of the men on the ground actually firing at us, all we had to do to cause them to flatten out on the ground was to fire a short burst from one of our machine guns. They had certainly been instilled with a fear of airplanes in our recent activities.

We saw several small concentrations of trucks, but the most important things we spotted were three large freight trains at the railroad station of the little town of Baides. All three of the trains were headed north, which gave additional proof that evacuation of that area was taking place on a large scale. When we returned to the field and reported our findings the squadron was ordered to get ready to bomb the station at Baides at once. Before we could complete our preparations, though, the weather had become so threatening that we couldn't take off. We sat around the field for the remainder of the day swearing at the weather and thinking of those three freight trains which we could almost visualize as steaming away to the northward and to safety.

At this time my motor was in very bad shape, throwing oil all over the fuselage and vibrating violently. Within ten minutes after a take-off my windshield would be too oil-smeared to see through. The only way I could keep my telescopic sight clean was to fly with the front of it covered up at all times except when it was actually being used. The vibration was probably due to the fact that I was still using the propeller with the two anti-aircraft holes in it. However, new propellers were scarce at the time, so there was nothing I could do but make the best of what I had.

The next morning was ideal for a bombing expedition, so we took off, hoping that at least one of the three freight trains would still be at the Baides railroad station. Imagine our surprise when we found all three of them still there! The only explanation I could think of was that when we flew over the day before we had been so low and so far back in their territory that they had assumed that it was a couple of their own planes prowling around. Joyfully we got into position and went to work. One of the trains started down the tracks at a good rate, but it had waited just a little too long. The bombs dropped by the first patrol landed all around its locomotive, which promptly blew up, causing the next few cars behind it to pile up in the wreckage and increase the confusion. The bombs dropped by my own and the third patrols landed all up and down the other two trains, which were side by side on the parallel tracks of a siding. The leader of the fourth patrol, though, failed to use his head and bombed the station itself, which was of no military importance at all. After dropping our bombs we began to fly up and down what was left of the three trains, strafing the uninjured portion of them with our machine guns.

All in all, I believe that that was the most destructive single flight our squadron ever made. We were in that vicinity only about twenty minutes, but when we left there it was a scene of desolation. At least half of the hundred-odd freight cars were either destroyed or burning. There were several tank cars, and we had concentrated on them with our incendiary bullets, with the result that most of them had caught fire and exploded, showering burning oil—probably gasoline—all over everything. We were finally forced to leave by the dense black clouds which began rolling up after the explosion of the tank cars; but by that time we had done just about all the damage that could be done. I doubt if a single car out of the entire three trains was salvaged intact.

The following day was one of the worst we ever had. It was extremely cold with a steady drizzle all day long. There was also a strong west wind blowing down from the snow-covered slopes of the Sierra Guadarrama which kept us shivering even when huddled around our fire. Late that afternoon we also had one of the worst hail and thunder storms of the year. When it ended there was at least three inches of ice covering the field. As it was obviously impossible to do any flying, I asked Jiménez for permission for my patrol to go into Madrid, and he very inconsiderately refused it. We explained that we merely wished to go in to the Hotel Florida for hot baths and that the sooner we started out the sooner we could get back. He said we were supposed to stay on the field until after sunset. We pointed out that the weather was so bad that it would be impossible even to tell when the sun set, much less try any flying, but that made no difference.

About that time Velasco, who was then leading the fourth patrol, came up and joined in the argument. He was rather short-tempered, so we soon had quite a rumpus started. He, my two trusty wing men and I introduced a new angle when we decided that Elias, the Russian interpreter, was as much to blame for the shortage of cars as Jiménez; then the fun really started. Spanish, Russian and American epithets of the most shocking and insulting variety were soon flying in all directions. It finally ended with Jiménez ordering us back to our planes. So we delivered a final broadside of our choicest phrases and retired, swearing, among other things, that we weren't going to take any more baths unless we were ordered to do so.

The following morning we were still feeling in more or less surly mood. It wasn't helped at all when Jiménez came out and ordered me to make a reconnaissance flight over a new section of the area back of the Guadalajara front and gave me an old frayed tourist's road map to navigate with. This flight took Justo and myself considerably northward of the area we were familiar with. Just as we got over the Sierra de las Cabras—Nanny-goat Mountains—the ceiling started dropping. The weather had been very threatening before we started, but we had taken off anyway and hoped for the best. When the ceiling kept on dropping we turned around and tried to get back over the mountains, but we had waited too long. All we could do was turn to the eastward and follow a highway along the northern slopes of the mountain range.

Then my very ancient road map frayed completely in two, and half of it blew out of the cockpit—the eastern half! However, we still had our road to follow. In fact we had no other choice than to follow it; the clouds had dropped so low that the surrounding mountaintops were already covered. And all this time we were far back in enemy territory! You can imagine my feelings; no map, in enemy territory, and the ceiling still on its way down. Luck was with us, however, and the road finally led us out over a less mountainous part of the country where the ceiling was at least stationary, though still dangerously low. I hadn't the faintest notion as to our position, so I set a course to the south-eastward toward what I knew to be our territory. We finally came out from under the clouds into bright sunlight over an extensive valley which I recognized as some part of the valley in which Albacete was located. I didn't know which part it was, but I finally spotted a small camouflaged landing field and we landed—on the last few drops of our gasoline—after more than two hours of continuous flying.

That particular field hadn't been used for some time, so there was no one there except the peasant caretaker. He informed us that we were about three miles east of the little town of Villanueva de la Jara, and that the field we had landed on was an emergency field which had been placed there for the very purpose we had used it for. This field turned out to be about 125 miles south-east of Guadalajara, our starting point, showing that we had covered quite a bit of territory. What hurt us worst of all was that we had to walk the three miles to town and the sun was blazing down. As we were dressed for near-freezing weather, we were extremely uncomfortable. In the village we were taken to the military commander of the local hospital, who had the only telephone in town. Justo took charge of it and went to work. He first called up Jiménez, told him where we were and asked him what we were to do. Jiménez told us to stay where we were and he would see to it that help was sent to us from Albacete, which was only a short distance to the south of us.

We waited around for the rest of the day, until the arrival of a

114

starter truck with a few gallons of oil and a couple of barrels of aviation gasoline. By the time we filled up, it was too late to start back to Guadalajara, so we decided to spend the night in town. The mayor took us under his wing and showed us over his domain. We were the first fighting-plane pilots ever to visit that particular town, so nothing would do but for us to visit all the leading citizens. And those people had the true spirit of southern hospitality. Whenever the *alcalde* took us into a house, there was no business of knocking; we just pushed the door open and walked into the house. All the houses were extremely old—as old as the town, I suppose—and were of heavy stone construction. Each one had a room especially designed for cooking over an open fire in the middle of the floor. The entire ceiling of one of these cooking rooms is built in the shape of an inverted funnel, so that the room is quite free of smoke. At each stop we were served with an excellent variety of local wine, which was evidently saved for special occasions. We ended our tour at the *alcalde*'s home, where we had supper in one of the cooking rooms I have described. As he had invited the head of the house at each of the places we visited, the little room was quite crowded.

Chairs were borrowed from various houses around the neighborhood, and we were seated around the sides of the room. The *alcalde*'s wife and two of his very good-looking daughters came in to prepare the meal. We were very fortunate in being able to observe the proceedings, which were all new to me.

One of the girls brought in a bundle of sticks and built a fire directly under the center of the inverted funnel, after which a large iron grid was placed over the fire. While she was doing this, her mother and the other girl brought in a huge pan and a freshly butchered kid. The mother immediately started cutting up the kid into small pieces, while the girl heated the pan, greased it, and rubbed garlic, onion and various unrecognizable seasonings around its inside. When this operation had been completed to the mother's satisfaction, the pan was placed over the fire and such portions of the goat as had already been cut up were thrown in, the remaining portions going in as soon as they could be dismembered.

All this time the men were sitting round drinking wine and talking. Justo, the *alcalde* and I were having a little conversation to ourselves near the fire, when all at once the alcalde pulled out a long, razor-edged clasp knife and opened it. He then leaned over and cut off the goat's scrotum and, still talking to us, nonchalantly proceeded to extract the testicles, split them open, wrap them in some sort of damp wrapping which one of the girls handed him, and pop them into the hot ashes beneath the pan. After about twenty minutes he raked them out and removed the now charred wrapping. Then, to my horror, he informed Justo and me that, as we were the honor guests, he bestowed the two choicest tidbits upon us.

While my stomach is usually strong enough for any emergency, it was in revolt at this sudden honor. Justo saved the day, though, by calling for additional condiments, thus giving me time to get used to the idea. This was accomplished by imagining that I had eaten nothing for at least a week. I then did such a good job of wolfing down my portion that the kind *alcalde* felt flattered. He informed Justo privately that he had never before seen anyone so obviously appreciative.

In the meantime the ladies had been keeping up the good work on the stewpan. After the goat meat had simmered for a while they started adding other ingredients, mostly vegetables, and additional seasoning. About an hour after the fire was laid, the *alcalde*'s wife announced that the meal was ready. The pan was removed from the grill and placed on the floor within easy reach of all the guests. The girls then came around and gave us each a sharp knife and a round, flat loaf of bread, about six inches in diameter—and not a sign of a plate. To make things worse, I couldn't even imagine what Emily Post would have advised doing in those circumstances.

However, good old Justo came to the rescue again and showed me how it was done. The trick was to spear a piece of meat or vegetable from the pan with the knife and place it on the loaf of bread, which you held on your lap. There it was further cut up and eaten with pieces of bread cut from the outer edge of the loaf. By the time you worked in to the center of the loaf it was thoroughly soaked in juice and was then consumed as a sort of dessert. The whole meal was washed down with a very good local wine, and it still lingers in my memory as one of the most satisfying I have ever had.

After the meal we sat around and talked until the fire went out; that is, the men sat around, but the women discreetly retired after clearing up the room. Then we were taken around to visit two or three houses which the *alcalde* had overlooked before; at each of these the inevitable wine was produced. Finally, we were taken back to the *alcalde*'s house and shown to our quarters for the night, after one of the best times we had had in many a day.

We were up before daylight the next morning and, after a glass of *café con leche* (coffee and goat's milk), went out to the field in a Russian pilot's car. His mechanics had already arrived there and had our planes warming up. The Russian pilot had brought along an excellent aviation map, so we were soon on our way back to Guadalajara. The change from the summer weather of the Júcar Valley to the winter weather of the Guadalajara Valley was just as startling as our outward-bound transition had been.

Jiménez was on hand to greet us as soon as we climbed out of our planes and immediately tried to bawl us out. We countered by climbing his frame for sending us out on a reconnaissance flight in threatening weather and with only a defective road map for a navigational chart. After which we parted on our usual amicable terms. My mechanic, by this time, had become accustomed to my spending an occasional night elsewhere, so he merely shrugged his shoulders and said with a grin, "*un céntimo malo siempre volverá*" (a bad penny always comes back). Before we left the field that night we had our planes loaded up with bombs for a projected before-daylight bombing expedition in the morning.

The next day I was ordered out on another reconnaissance flight. Again Justo accompanied me, but this time we were given an excellent aviation map of the area we were to scout. We found hardly a sign of life anywhere back of the Guadalajara front. Two little towns had anti-aircraft guns which fired a few optimistic shots at us, but aside from that there was absolutely nothing to report. No troops moving, no trucks in sight, all railroads deserted. I suppose that our recent raid at least had the effect of speeding up the Italian evacuation of that territory. José seemed very pleased to hear my report and hinted that we might soon have something more interesting to do. Later events proved that he knew what he was talking about.

CHAPTER X

SKY WORK OVER MADRID

On the morning of April ninth we started off with a bang on what turned out to be a fake offensive on the front directly outside of Madrid. Our squadron again had the duty of signaling the beginning of the attack by dropping bombs at the right time, 8:30 in the morning, and then strafing the enemy trenches located in the area known as the Casa de Campo. We loaded up with bombs and took off, arriving over Madrid right on the dot. There was just the right amount of clouds, so we managed to get over our objective without attracting any anti-aircraft fire or enemy planes. Then down we went, one patrol after the other, and did an excellent job of bombing. We came out of our dive almost due west of the center of the city and made a left turn over it to avoid enemy anti-aircraft fire. However, as we swooped over the city our own gunners opened up on us; evidently someone had failed to warn them, but fortunately they scored no hits.

We then made a wide circle around the city while climbing back to our original altitude. Then we started diving down on the enemy trenches at Casa de Campo; this time, one plane after the other. The enemy anti-aircraft batteries had come to life by that time; they only had about two emplacements but even at that, by the time we made our third machine-gunning round we were flying through clouds of little shell bursts; also a hail of anti-aircraft machine gun bullets, whose tracers we could see very plainly. There were too many bullets that we could see to worry about. After our third pass at the trenches Jiménez re-formed the squadron and we flew back to the field, where José soon made his appearance and congratulated us for doing such excellent work.

That afternoon at 5:30 we took off and repeated our performance of the morning. This time there wasn't a cloud in the sky and there was considerably more anti-aircraft fire. We also had the disadvantage of having the sun very low in the west over enemy territory, so that enemy planes would have been very hard to see coming from that direction. Since none of them made their appearance, though, we carried out our mission as per schedule. We did our bombing and machine-gunning a little further south than we had in the morning. This time there was so much anti-aircraft fire that after each dive we would cut back over the city much lower than before—lower than the tops of the taller buildings, in fact—and we wouldn't start climbing until we were well past the centre of the city. I usually started my climb right over the huge bull ring, which was Madrid's best aerial landmark.

The most remarkable thing I noticed while flying over the city was the large number of spectators taking in the show. The knights of old have had many a large gallery for their tournaments in Madrid, but they never had any that could compare with the one we had. Madrid, at that time, had a population of approximately 1,200,000, at least half of them were on housetops, in the windows of the taller buildings, and out in the open streets. The fact that the air was full of shrapnel and bullets didn't seem to bother them at all. When we swished around a tall building we naturally drew the enemy's anti-aircraft bursts along with us but, as far as I could see, the people on top of the buildings weren't paying any attention to them.

Some enterprising newsreel cameraman could certainly have made a scoop taking pictures of that exhibition. An entire squadron of fighting-planes weaving along the trenches, one after the other, with machine guns hammering away; the shrieking and whining of wind through struts and flying wires; the outraged roads of motors protesting at the bottoms of dives; the sharp, hollow-sounding explosions of anti-aircraft shells; the heavy, rivet-machine-like pounding of fifty-caliber anti-aircraft machine guns, all intermingled with the cheering and shrieking of the enthusiastic spectators, would have supplied sound effects that no Hollywood studio could duplicate. As we roared past the taller buildings we could see people jumping up and down and waving everything they could lay hands on. Of course, we couldn't hear the cheering; our planes were making too much noise, but we could almost feel the waves of acclamation emanating from them. If they could only have seen their heroes— faces covered with grease and whiskers, clothes soaked with perspiration! But that was the first day they had seen their own planes in action in two months, and the planes were giving the *criminales fachosos* hell. We naturally returned to the field feeling very pleased with ourselves. Most of the planes in the squadron had either shrapnel or bullet holes in them, but none of the pilots were injured.

The next day we made three more flights up to Madrid and pulled off the same stunts. Everything went off well except that our blundering fourth patrol dropped its bombs in our own lines on the first trip. The leader of the offending patrol, Velasco, was so obviously heartbroken that we tried to cheer him up by telling him he might only have hit the anti-aircraft battery which had fired on us the day before; but he was despondent for several days afterward.

The enemy must have rushed up more anti-aircraft guns during the night, because there were about twice as many shell bursts at a time as there were the day before. How we all managed to get through it safely I don't know, for all our planes were full of shrapnel holes by the time the day's work was over. All pilots, though, were still intact and unpunctured. The only ones who weren't entirely happy at the end of the day were the mechanics. They had to work overtime that night slapping patches over holes in fabric.

The thirteenth of April turned out to be a pretty fair day for flying—although the field was still rather wet. At 9:30 in the morning Justo and I took off on another one of our reconnaissance flights back of the Guadalajara front. This time there were a few signs of enemy activity; on one road we spotted a group of six enemy tanks, of Italian make, headed toward Madrid. When I made my report at Alcalá, José seemed more interested in the tanks than in anything else. At 3 o'clock that afternoon the entire squadron took off with bombs to see if we could locate the tanks. They had made good their escape, but we did find a concentration of trucks—which we bombed and machine-gunned enthusiastically.

Just after releasing my bombs during my first dive on the trucks I felt something give the plane an awful jar. At first I thought it had been caused by a burst of anti-aircraft beneath the plane, but upon looking back I could see no tell-tale smoke puffs, so I paid no more attention to the incident. When I got back to the field I discovered that my luck was still holding up—one of my right bombs had struck my right forward stabilizer strut and snapped it completely in two. Fortunately, the bomb hadn't exploded, but it was a wonder that the tail assembly hadn't been shaken to pieces in the dives and pull-outs which followed the bombardment dive. The cause of this unusual accident was that I had been in too steep a dive when I released the bombs and had also been in a slight skid to the right.

Later in the afternoon a brilliant red Lockheed transport came in and landed on the field. A few minutes later a car came over to my patrol with its pilot, and to my great surprise he turned out to be an American. He was Lieutenant Rose-Marie, whose wife had been at Albacete when Whitey and I went there after taking off in that thunderstorm. We had a great time talking over the war in general and Spanish aviation in particular. As neither of us had had very much opportunity to talk English, we were both only too glad when the weather kept all planes grounded the next day. Our spare time was spent in watching the many truck and bus load of our troops passing through from the Guadalajara front to other more lively fronts. Late that afternoon the weather cleared up enough for Rose-Marie to take off and be on his way to Albacete.

At high noon on the fifteenth we received surprise orders to go to the pilots' house and pack a small bag with our toilet articles and sufficient linen for a week's absence. After we had our luggage stowed in our planes, we were informed that we were to go to the Teruel front and help out for a while. The Russian squadron from Alcalá was going along, so we all met above a large table-topped hill south of Alcalá and started out for Teruel. After an hour and forty minutes of cross-country flying we landed on a fine, large, dry field just outside of a small town, Sarrión. Its only drawback was that it was very hot and dusty. It was about fifteen miles from Teruel and sixty from Valencia.

There was another squadron of biplane fighters there when we landed and it didn't take long to discover that it was Baumler's squadron under the command of Kosokov. Baumler must have had advance word of our coming, because he was over to see me almost before my plane had stopped rolling. He told me that we were getting ready to start a big offensive against Teruel. That was the reason for our two-day fake offensive at Madrid—to draw Franco's attention away from the Teruel front.

I asked Baumler if he had found out anything concerning Chang's whereabouts, but he was just as much in the dark as I was. He had seen LaCalle only about a week or so before and had inquired about Chang—but hadn't been able to learn anything. LaCalle had said that he didn't know where Chang was, but thought that he might have gone to Japan for a rest period. He wasn't at all sure about it, though.

That evening, when our squadron went into Sarrión, we found out that we were entirely unexpected by the local commissary department. They didn't even have a place for us to sleep, but thought there might be some cots coming in from Valencia shortly after midnight. The evening meal was also a trifle scanty, on account of one squadron's provisions having to be stretched out to take care of three squadrons. By way of venting our rage at the commissary's unpreparedness and also to celebrate our reunion, Baumler and I purchased three bottles of rather doubtful Málaga wine. By the time we had polished off the third bottle my indignation had become so great that I flatly refused to wait until after midnight for a cot, and bedded down in the back seat of a new V-8 sedan which happened to be in a nearby garage.

The next morning we were routed out at 4:30, and as soon as we could get washed up at the local horse trough we were hauled out to the field and given instructions to load up with bombs and stand by. Then Jiménez came around with a large map and showed us the lay of the land. Our front lines encircled Teruel on three sides, somewhat in the shape of a wide-mouthed bottle, with the next extending out to the northwest along two railroad tracks and a highway. We were to bomb along one side of this bottleneck and then fly protection for a squadron of our Rasantes which were to come over with heavier bombs and their ground-strafing machine guns. Everything worked out well, both our bombardment and that of the Rasantes being right on our respective objectives. Shortly after the Rasantes left the scene, three of our Katiuskas came over and dropped a few heavy bombs for good measure. There wasn't a sign of any enemy anti-aircraft fire or fighting-planes. We returned to the field expecting to eat a hearty breakfast, but the commissary department was still disorganized, so all we could do was sit around and drink water.

At 10:30 we took off and did the same thing over again; but this time we had a little opposition. One of the patrols of Kosokov's squadron ran into a patrol of Heinkel fighters and had a slight brush with them. They dog-fought for about ten minutes, and each patrol managed to shoot down one of the other side's planes. The Heinkels very wisely dived away and went home when the rest of the squadron made its appearance on the scene. We found that Kosokov had lost one of his new replacements—a young Spaniard named Tuya—who had been shifted from our squadron to his before we left the Madrid front.

At 3 o'clock that afternoon we got our first meal of the day, and it was brought out to the various patrols in large baskets. It consisted of some very hard bread, some equally hard native ham, two hard-boiled eggs apiece and two bottles of wine apiece. When we finished that we were still just as hungry as we were before we started. Flying gives one a ravenous appetite and we were accustomed to the enormous meals we had been getting up at the Madrid front. We were feeling rather down at the mouth when we received orders to get all set for another bombardment flight at 4:45 sharp. Even the fact that we did our best bombardment work of the day on that flight failed to make us feel any more kindly toward the commissary department. That night, though, they edged back into favor, or at least tolerance, by giving us a really excellent meal and having enough beds go around.

All was not going well with our squadron. Jiménez, though a fine individual pilot, was not the aerial leader that LaCalle had been. All our pilots had seen him get us into situations where, if

124

we had been attacked, we would have been helpless. The fact that we weren't attacked made no difference; the pilots knew it anyway. So, on this night, we had a showdown. Velasco, leader of the fourth patrol, made a formal protest, backed by all the rest of the Spanish pilots in the squadron, and asked for reinstatement of LaCalle as squadron leader. Kosokov, who was technically in command of the three squadrons at the field, was the recipient of the protest and he issued a Portia-like decree. He said that Jiménez would continue to be in command of the squadron on the ground, while I, as the senior remaining pilot, would command it in the air. I had taken no part in the argument—in fact, I wasn't present—so the final decision was rather a surprise to me. My two wing men came and communicated the news to me, and as it seemed to be the general decision of the squadron, I accepted the nomination.

The seventeenth of April turned out to be our big day on the Teruel front. On that day we had our only general dogfight and saw our last sight of enemy fighting-planes on that front. Our first flight of the day was uneventful, but on the second we really had to work for our money. This was the most evenly matched combat we had been in, up to that time; there were twenty-one enemy fighters and eighteen of us—three six-plane squadrons. Their planes were new Heinkels, 1936 model, while ours were of the Boeing P-12 type, about 1930 model.

This fight was so interesting that I will give a straight description of it from start to finish.

It was a nice, warm, sunny day, without a cloud in the sky, and most of us were lying in the shade of our plane wings. All at once I heard a pair of dull, thudding reports and as I jumped up I saw two red flares soaring up from the field house—our emergency signal! Getting into my parachute, clambering into the plane and starting my motor was only a matter of seconds. A few more seconds and my wing men, Justo and Magrinán, were likewise all set and off we went. I circled the field once, to give the third patrol a chance to tail on, and then started climbing. Jiménez's plane had a broken gas line, so the first patrol never even got off the ground. Thus I had only six planes to work with.

I hadn't the slightest idea what the emergency might be, but I lined out for Teruel full blast, climbing all the time. We arrived over Teruel at an altitude of about 13,000 feet and saw—nothing. However, upon going past the city a mile or two, I spotted one of our Katiuska bombers coming toward us from the opposite direction. And was it coming! You could see that it was being urged along by both straining motors and the will power of its occupants. Smoke was coming from each motor, and the plane was in a slight dive; it was all we could do to catch up with the thing.

Putting all these indications together, I came to the conclusion that the Katiuska had run into something that its crew didn't approve of, and that they might feel better with a squadron of fighting-planes to help them across the lines. I therefore reversed our course and started to fly the usual protection over the Katiuska's tail. Then, as we came past Teruel, I saw the enemy. They were away to our right—in three echelons of seven planes each. Their lowest echelon was about 10,000 feet up, while their highest was at least 13,000. Their third echelon was almost exactly halfway between the other two.

At the same time I saw the enemy planes, I saw a patrol of our own planes closing in on the lowest of the enemy echelons. Other patrols of ours were coming in from behind, heading for the middle echelon. By that time our Katiuska was safely across the lines, so I made a right turn and headed for the third and highest of the enemy echelons. As we swung around the turn I put my planes into battle formation and went into a slight dive by way of picking up extra speed, a very handy thing to have in an aerial encounter.

Such was the general layout just before the combat. The enemy planes—Heinkels—were a mile or more south of Teruel; one patrol of three of our planes was about to attack their lowest echelon; three more of our patrols—nine planes—were coming up from the south; and my outfit of six planes was diving into the fray from the east, with the morning sun at our backs. I don't think the enemy even saw my outfit at all until it was too late to do anything about it.

I was about two thirds of a mile away when our first patrol went into action against the first enemy echelon. There was a fierce scramble for a few seconds, then two of the Heinkels came wavering out of the mixture. They immediately went into their final spins and splattered against the terrain a couple of miles below. Then one of our planes came wavering out, caught itself for a moment, came around and up in a sharp left chandelle, and collided head on with an enemy plane. Even in the bright sunlight the explosion was blinding in its intensity. Then there was nothing to be seen of the two except a few large objects dropping earthward and a few fragments of wings and tail surfaces going down slowly, turning over and over like pieces of cardboard thrown from a high window.

At this point the three of our patrols coming up from the south went into action against the second—and what remained of the first—of the enemy echelons. This left only their third echelon to contend with, so I took my crew over and closed in with them.

After that, things were happening too fast even to see what was going on in our own private little dogfight. Most of our physical movements were being made automatically, and our mental decisions and observations were being made—and forgotten—on the spur of the moment. My entire picture of that phase of the battle was framed in the glass of my machine gun sight. Here, however, are a few of the impressions I jotted down immediately after we landed.

Our entering charge breaks up the precise, military echelon of the enemy planes. I waggle my wings—our break-up signal—and we close in on individual planes. There is a mad whirl of planes going round and round. Planes start sliding across my sight—at first only greenish ones with black emblems—each getting a burst of machine gun fire; and then, as the affair becomes more intimate, planes of both sides slide across so that caution becomes necessary to keep from firing on one's own planes. We have to be careful not to bank too violently or we "black out"; that is, the centrifugal force draws the blood away from our heads and sight dims to complete blackness unless the pressure is eased. To black out completely in a dogfight is almost certain death.

I see a green plane turning in toward me and I automatically pull over to meet it. I get in line first, and open fire, steadily this time. Although my adversary never succeeds in getting in line, I see his machine guns winking away and his tracers dripping blobs of smoke—as I suppose he sees mine—but he is just a trifle too late.

Metal starts flying from the left side of his motor, followed by water and black smoke. Then a line of fabric tatters works down the sleek side of the plane. As he goes past, his plane is in a sort of sliding roll, and is already headed for the ground, leaving a long, thin trail of the unmistakable greasy black smoke. (I remember wishing at this time that someone was off in the distance taking motion pictures, so that I could see what a dog-fight really looks like; you can't seen an entire fight when you are in it). We are still tangled up with a few Heinkels, so once more I start handing out short bursts, first here and then there. I get behind one of the Heinkels and am just getting lined up for the kill when one of them gets behind my plane. Fortunately, out of the corner of my eye, I see the familiar tracer streaks just off to the right and pull around in a violent vertical bank to the left. A close call! The Heinkel either can't follow or doesn't dare to, and continues on down in his dive.

I look around and note with relief that all my men are still intact and doing well. The Heinkels have got tired of playing and are diving for ground as fast as they can get clear. They can out-dive us, but we follow and fire until they get out of range.

At this point more or less coherent thought started again. I saw that we had plenty of men below, so I pulled up and organized my formation again at 5,000 feet. There was no need of it, though, as the only enemy planes in sight were two who were cornered in a little valley below by about five of Kosokov's men. These two were polished off as I watched—they didn't have a chance. The valley had sides that were just high enough to eliminate any chance of the two unfortunate Heinkels being able to climb out, and our planes could outclimb them; so all they could do was fly around in the little valley until they were shot down. You can't even surrender in an airplane; your opponent wouldn't know whether you were joking or not.

We flew around for awhile then went back to the field and awaited reports from our front line observation posts. And what reports we received! There were five of the Heinkels down on our side of the lines and three more had been seen to crash on their side. Our loss was only one plane and that was the one which collided at the start of the fray.

That collision should become one of the epics of aerial warfare. Enough of the remains of the two planes and pilots fell to ground for the medical authorities to determine that the enemy pilot had been the squadron commander and that our own pilot—a young Spaniard named Calvo—had been shot through the neck, his jugular vein being severed. His maneuvers prior to the collision showed very plainly what had happened. The bullet through his neck had momentarily dazed him; that was when the plane was wavering and falling. Then he recovered his faculties and, upon seeing that his end was near—because even if he had put his plane into a full-power dive he would have bled to death before reaching the ground—he deliberately pulled up and rammed the enemy plane before passing out altogether. A really heroic gesture!

Several of our planes were shot up in the fight, but all of them, except Calvo's, managed to get back to the field under their own power. One of the new replacements in Kosokov's squadron came back with his plane absolutely riddled, but he escaped without a scratch. He informed his mechanic that he had smelled something burning at one time while in the air, and when the mechanic investigated he found that an incendiary bullet had passed through both sides of the cockpit. A string pulled taut through both of the holes showed that the bullet must have passed right under the pilot's nose—and was probably what he had smelled burning. Kosokov took one scowling look at the plane and immediately grounded the pilot—because all the bullets had come from the rear. He reasoned that the pilot must have spent most of his time running away from enemy planes, or some of the many bullets would have come from the front. My own plane had four or five bullet holes out at the end of the front wing, proving that I hadn't swung away from those tracers any too soon.

At 2:15 that afternoon we took off without bombs to protect a squadron of Rasantes. This time there wasn't a sign of an enemy plane. Our Rasantes did an excellent job of bombing and strafing the enemy trenches, and when they got through we went down and did a little strafing on our own hook. While we were engaged in this pastime, we saw our first enemy anti-aircraft fire on that front. A lone anti-aircraft gun opened up and fired an occasional shell. Its aim was so atrocious, though, that we paid no attention to it.

That night we all gathered at the local tavern and celebrated our victory. We also found out, from the front line observers, why we had had such an easy time with the Heinkels. They were brand new, built in late 1936. The pilot of every one of those new Heinkels had been a new Spanish pilot, with no previous combat experience at all. Even their squadron commander had been flying for only four months, mostly at a training school, while most of our men were veteran combat pilots. It must have been some experiment or other on Franco's part. At any rate we drank up all the champagne in Sarrión and then went to work on the local wines—thus assuring ourselves a good throbbing headache apiece the following morning.

On April nineteenth we really went to work in earnest. We figured out a relief system so that no more than one six-plane group of us would have to go out at a time. Then a regular procession of our Rasante squadrons started coming over at half-hour intervals. As each squadron passed over the field, one of our six-plane groups would take off and escort it up to the front. Thus, there were planes either taking off or landing all day long—with never a sign of enemy fighting-planes.

Late that afternoon three of our Katiuskas passed over the field heading toward the front. Shortly after that we heard the detonations of their heavy bombs going off, and then saw a huge column of smoke start rising from the direction of Teruel. They had evidently struck either a fuel or an ammunition depot. When I flew over the city on my last flight of the day, smoke was still rising from buildings near its eastern boundary walls. We finished our day's work by bombing in and around the village of Villarquemado.

The next day we resumed our original squadron formations and stood by. At high noon we escorted two squadrons of

Rasantes over the lines, and they bombed the stuffing out of the little town of Celadas and the trenches around it. There was a layer of clouds not more than 3000 feet up, so we were forced to stay down fairly low. We could easily see our tanks lined up and ready to follow up the bombardment. As soon as the first of the bombs hit the ground, they started out on their charge. When we returned to the field, Kosokov and his boys went up with some more Rasantes, and then we all went up and flew patrol over Teruel while our ground troops captured Celadas. It must have been a pretty good show, but by that time there was too much smoke over the vicinity for us to be able to see very much.

On the twenty-first we had absolutely nothing to do except sit around in the shade of our plane wings from 4:30 in the morning until after 7 that night. Fortunately, I managed to discover a very vicious centipede under some rocks in an adjoining field. By putting two of them into a glass jar and teasing them, we could get them into a fighting rage, and then they would tear into each other. They were about four inches long, with powerful jaws, and seemed to be a trifle poisonous. They were also very hard to kill; the winner in one of their fights always bit off the head of the loser, but that made no difference to the headless one; he would keep on crawling around anyway, head or no head. These fights would last for at least half an hour and whenever one ended quite a few pesetas changed hands. I never did find any of these centipedes anywhere else, so they must have been peculiar to that locality.

We escorted nine Rasantes up to the front the next morning and watched them work on Villarquemado and vicinity. By this time the enemy had installed several batteries of anti-aircraft guns, which kept us pretty busy dodging around. That afternoon they gave us a different type of mission—machine-gunning artillery emplacements. A certain emplacement just outside of a little town called Caudete had been giving a lot of trouble, so all our fighting-planes were ordered out to work on it and we did it with a vengeance. While some of us would be up above, flying protection, the remainder would be down below strafing the offending gunners. There were about eight anti-aircraft guns popping away at us, but they never placed any of their bursts closer than 300 feet from any of our planes. The guns we were after were placed in the side of a little hill, right over a creek, and were so cleverly camouflaged that we had trouble locating them at first. After they had finally been located, though, it was just a matter of diving down on them and holding the gun trips forward. When we returned to the field we learned that we had succeeded in silencing at least half of the offending battery, which wasn't so bad. After that, we wound up the day's work by herding another squadron of Rasantes up to the front and back.

About noon that day something occurred which thoroughly enraged all of us older pilots. We had all been nursing our old crates along, crying for new planes to replace them, and on this particular day the first one of the new replacement planes was sent to us. A very inexperienced Spanish pilot had been assigned to the job of ferrying it to our field from the assembly plant back of Los Alcázares. When he arrived, he circled the field once, tried to land downwind, and very naturally overshot, as the wind was blowing rather hard at the time. He then made two more unsuccessful passes with the same result, and finally decided to land anyway, still in the same downwind direction. He came in like the proverbial bat out of hell, drifted all the way across the field, and crashed head on into Magrinán's plane, which was parked about a hundred yards from mine. The pilot, as is usually the case in such incidents, was merely scratched, while both planes were total wrecks. Magrinán wanted to shoot the pilot and had my official approval both as patrol and as squadron leader, but Justo kept his head and took Magrinán's gun away from him. That poor pilot wished that he had been shot, though, when Kosokov came up and found out what had happened.

To make things worse, when we came in from machine-gunning the artillery emplacements that afternoon, two of our pilots, Velasco and Lecha, tried to land crosswind and washed out their respective landing gears. That made a total of four planes out of commission in one day on our field; and all on account of pilot trouble.

Kosokov's own mother would have hesitated to speak to him after these last two incidents. Of course, the wind had been both violent and variable, but that field was so dusty at all times that there should have been no difficulty at all about telling its direction. Baumler and I both agreed, with much profanity, that the Fascists were foolish to fight us in the air when, if we were left alone, we did a much better job of destroying our planes on our own landing fields.

It was certainly a picturesque scene in our mess room that night. Kosokov and two other Russians were squabbling at one end of the table—in Russian. Baumler and I were cursing a blue streak in American at the other end; while Jiménez, Velasco and other assorted Spaniards were shouting at each other across the center section of the table—in Spanish. And the mechanics, by way of adding variety, were having a spirited argument at their own table in various and sundry provincial dialects. Chamorro, my chief mechanic, was holding forth in his native Asturian dialect. He was pointing out, with more vehemence than accuracy—considering Chang's various accidents—that no pilot in his patrol had ever cracked up a plane, and that if it hadn't been for that blankety-blank ferry pilot, no plane in his patrol would ever have cracked up. I think all our bad temper that night was due to the fact that these aggravating incidents had caught us after several days of very hard work, when our nerves were on edge. I have observed the same phenomenon among seamen after weathering several days of stormy weather. Anyway, we were all on the verge of getting into a general argument when the commissary officer saved the day by bringing in a case of very good champagne and changing the subject to the dogfight of a couple of days before.

CHAPTER XI

A "QUIET" FURLOUGH

It was a rather strange sight, at this period, to see the little children of our village going to school just as though there wasn't a war anywhere nearer than China. They were laughing and chattering so loudly that it was only occasionally that you could hear the Government's siege guns hammering away against the walls of Teruel about fifteen miles to the northward. I took advantage of a slack day to look in at the village blacksmith's place of business. It was evidently just as it had always been for the last three or four centuries. The air for the forge was supplied by a huge cowhide bellows motivated by the blacksmith's eight-year-old apprentice. All the rest of the equipment was in keeping with the bellows—including the blacksmith. He knew how to use what equipment he had, though, and was turning out plowshare points with amazing rapidity and skill, in spite of his bulk and deceptively slow movements.

An old man was sitting outside of one house with a large panful of wheat kernels, from which he was painstakingly removing spoiled grains. He accepted the Russian cigarette which I offered him, but he didn't seem to think very much of it. He seemed to be entirely uninterested in the war, but this was evidently because he thought he knew what the outcome would be. He informed me, in Valenciano dialect, that the Government would take care of the war, and that there were a lot of other things to do besides actually fighting in the trenches. He had me there; I hadn't thought of it in that way before.

Just before we knocked off, one evening, we received word to be ready to leave the next day. Evidently our work had been finished on that front. So that night we packed our few belongings in our handbags and had a farewell dinner with the local militia officers.

We took off at 6 o'clock sharp the next morning, and two hours later we landed on our old field at Campo X. The first thing I did there was to start my plane on its way through a general overhaul, which it certainly needed. Then I went over to the count's house and paid a visit to the sewing room where I found María and Cristina still in charge. They were overjoyed at my safe return, as they had heard that an American pilot had been killed at Teruel. I assured them that it had been a South American, and neither Baumler nor myself. Chang's girl friend, Cristina, asked me about him, but I didn't know any more about his whereabouts than she did. I noticed, however, when I visited the pilots' house in Azuqueca, that all his personal effects were still there.

It was certainly good to get back the comforts of our house in Azuqueca. That afternoon I walked from the field to the village with the two girls and visited with them until just before the start of our evening meal. By that time I had become so used to speaking in Spanish that I had even started thinking in Spanish— broken Spanish, anyway—and carrying on a conversation in that language was easier than talking in English. I was somewhat surprised, though, when I discovered that neither of the two girls had the slightest desire to go to America. I was laboring under the delusion that all Europeans wanted to come to America and would do so at the slightest opportunity. But María, at least, had no desire to live anywhere except in Spain, even though there was a war going on there.

The following day LaCalle came over to Campo X to see how we were getting along. I took advantage of the occasion to ask him about Chang, but he was unable even to guess where he might be. At that time there were only four of us left out of the original twelve pilots who started out with the squadron. So, when LaCalle saw our weary faces, he decreed that we should get a week's leave apiece. The four of us left were "Chato" Casteneda, Ortiz, Gil and myself. LaCalle offered us our choice of either going to Madrid or staying in Azuqueca for our week of leisure. Chato had a girl friend in Azuqueca, so he elected to stay there; the other three of us packed up and motored in to Madrid, where we took rooms at the Florida Hotel.

As I hadn't heard any direct news from the United States in over a month, I lost no time in locating the Americans who were staying there. They were mostly newspaper people—Matthews, of the New York Times; Martha Gellhorn, with Hearst, I think; Ernest Hemingway, novelist; Gorrell, of the United Press; and others—but there were also a few members of the Lincoln Brigade there. At the time of my arrival they were all congregated in Hemingway's room on the second floor. Hemingway was to leave for Paris the following day, and they were throwing some sort of farewell party in his honor.

The conversation was just getting well launched when I heard a shrill, whistling sound—followed by a loud explosion and a lot of clattering. I jumped up and went over to the window—and discovered that a shell had struck the decorative top of the Paramount Theater just across the plaza—the Plaza de Callao—from the hotel. I looked questioningly at the others. "Oh, that's only the beginning of the usual afternoon bombardment," said one; and the conversation continued as before. The only one who paid any attention at all to the explosions was a young cameraman, who dashed out to see if he could get any pictures of shell landings.

The little group included the commanding officer and the medical officer of the Lincoln Brigade. They informed me the shells usually come over in groups of three, and that the proper thing to do, if caught out on the streets, was step into a doorway of a store. All buildings in Madrid are of heavy stone construction, so that sounded logical enough. I had already seen many buildings which had been struck by shells, and they had been just barely nicked.

My Lincoln Brigade friends also warned me to be careful about traveling around the principal thoroughfares during the *siesta* period—from high noon to 3:30 or 4 in the afternoon. I thought this a rather strange precaution, but didn't want to display my ignorance by asking questions. I rather suspected that they might be leading me on into the trap of a catch question. Later on, I had good reason for wishing I had asked a few questions.

I soon became accustomed to the occasional trios of shells whistling over from Franco's territory, and started into the usual rounds of Madrid's social activities. These were fairly extensive, as the war hadn't affected the city's night life at all. And in the daytime there are some of the most interesting sights in the world to be seen there, even in peacetime. My favorite daytime occupation was visiting the front line trenches, which could easily be reached without the least danger. There it was possible to look through loopholes and actually see enemy trenches only a short distance away. I even did a little still hunting while visiting the trenches—holding a rifle and trying to catch an unwary Fascist exposed. I never did see any of them exposed in their first-line trench, but you could get an occasional long shot at one of them farther back. Whether I hit any of them is a matter of conjecture but, considering my squirrel-hunting training down in the wilds of Arkansas, I should say that the odds were about even. The newly-trained Spanish militiamen were not very good rifle shots, so the Fascists were a little careless in the rear of the trenches and I got several good steady shots. The militia officers were very hospitable with their Fascist targets—any visitor to the trenches could be sure of being invited to take a few shots across the lines.

During my week in Madrid I attended two banquets. The first was given in honor of General Miaja, and the second was in honor of the aviation branch of the People's Army. On both these occasions I was the only English-speaking person present, so I could understand only parts of the speeches made. The orators were always either Spanish or Russian. General Miaja was present on both of these occasions and honored us with speeches. But, inasmuch as my hastily-acquired Spanish was good only for ordinary conversations, I don't know, to this day, what he talked about. As the food and entertainments were excellent on both occasions, however, I managed to have a pretty good time.

I took advantage of my stay in Madrid to have the final fittings of my new lower teeth made. The dentist was beginning to get a little worried about the daily shellings, so I thought that I had better get it over with before he decided to leave town. On the morning of the twenty-seventh a shell had struck the building just across the street from his office and had broken all of his front windows. So the day after that he made the final delivery and I found that he had done an extraordinarily good job of fitting.

From the third day of my furlough to the last I was almost driven to believe that the Fascists knew more about my activities than I did myself. On the third day I went up to my room after the noon meal and discovered that a three-inch shell had made a direct hit on my bathroom, completely wrecking it and part of the adjoining bedroom. Fragments had riddled my largest handbag and completely ruined a perfectly good electric razor and an almost new Graflex camera. But, worst of all, I had had two bottles of good Scotch whisky—the last two in the city, I think—hidden behind the bathtub, and they also were completely demolished. That gave me my first real personal grudge to settle with those Vandals across the lines. I was so enraged by the incident that I was still rather fluently cursing the Fascists when I went below to see the management about getting another room. I even went so far as to forget that other people might be able to understand English, until I was reminded of this fact by Miss Gellhorn, who happened to be sitting in the lobby at the time. However, she had been in Madrid long enough to know how it was, so she graciously accepted my apology. I waited until another shell whistled over, and then sprinted across the street to the corner bar-room, which happened to have beer on tap at that time. The shell in my room had one good result, though; the management moved me down to the second floor on the safe side of the building.

The following day Franco planted another shell right through the sidewalk in front of my favorite lobby window. I was in the habit of spending quite a lot of time every day sitting by this window, either reading or looking at the natives going by on the street. The shell failed to explode, which saved the life of a newspaper vendor who had his wares laid out on the window ledge. It went completely through the pavement and lodged about three feet under the surface, throwing pieces of cement all over that vicinity, breaking three of the four big lobby windows, and giving the newsboy, who was standing about five feet from where it hit the sidewalk, a choice collection of scratches and bruises. On this occasion I happened to be across the street in the Paramount Theater marveling at the fact that Popeye and Mickey Mouse could speak better Spanish than I could.

My last day in Madrid explained why my Lincoln Brigade friends had warned me to stay off the streets during the *siesta* period. It is the custom in Spain, and in Madrid especially, to have a meal in one place and then go somewhere else to have coffee. I supposed they follow that custom because it kills more time.

I had been running around Madrid with a Spanish girl named Dolores, to whom I had been introduced by Justo. Anyway, on this last day Dolores and I had lunch together at the Florida Hotel and then walked about three hundred yards up the Gran Vía to the Hotel Gran Vía for coffee. While there I managed to talk the head waiter into selling me a couple of bottles of champagne. When we finished our coffee we went out on the street and started to walk back to the Florida. Just as we were about halfway between the two hotels, we heard the first of the warning whistles; and it was right in the middle of the *siesta* period. All the stores along the Gran Vía were closed and had heavy iron screens rolled down their fronts, making one long canyon out of the street, and leaving us with no convenient doorways to duck into. All we could do was stand there with our mouths full of teeth. I have an idea that if there had been any spectators they could have seen question marks—comic-strip style—over each of our thick skulls.

The first shell struck the Paramount Building—which was about a hundred yards ahead of us—showering the street with pieces of cement and shell fragments; and all we could do was stand there. After all, there was no place which was any better than the spot we were standing on already, both of the hotels being too far away to get to before the next shell came over. Another ululating whistle and—Burrroooom!—this one struck the towering Telephone building just across the street from us. It was close enough to set us both back on our heels and shower us with stone fragments. The entire street filled up with the most remarkable combination of dust and smoke that I have ever seen. I thought for a minute that it might have been a gas shell.

At this point Dolores showed both her Spanish thrift and her presence of mind by taking one of the bottles of champagne from under my badly shaking left arm. Strangely enough, though, the very nearness of this shell rather cheered us up. We figured that if the Fascists could come that close to us without fatal results, they couldn't get us at all. Even the Spaniards have heard of the old saying about lightning never striking twice in the same place. Then the third and last shell came over. It struck the front of the Gran Vía Hotel—about three stories above the sidewalk—and showered the doorway we had just come out of with large chunks of stone cornice. We huddled against a building until it became apparent that no more shells were coming over and then, with unspoken mutual consent, hurried down to the Florida bar to settle our very unsteady nerves with double brandies and sodas.

Later that afternoon Dolores and I went over to the still-operating Paramount Theater to see Charlie Chaplin in *Tiempos Modernos*. At about the middle of the show three more shells came over, and two of them struck the building in the upper stories. As the building vibrated violently and a little plaster fell from the ceiling, I expected to see a riot begin at once; but not a bit of it! A few muffled curses from my nearest neighbours— directed against the *criminales fachosos*—were the only outward manifestations that anything out of the ordinary had occurred; and the audience was at least 50 per cent women and children. I didn't know whether to attribute their indifference to familiarity or to Charlie's personal appeal.

All those shellings of Madrid were really not doing a great amount of damage, so far as I could see. The buildings, as mentioned before, are all of heavy stone construction, so that unless a window is hit, the damage can be repaired in a couple of days. The principal damage occurs when they shell the residential districts of the civilian population. There a six- or eight-inch shell could completely demolish a residence and wipe out all its occupants—usually old men, women or children, as most of the able-bodied men were up in the trenches.

The attitude of those Madrid civilians was certainly amazing; I would never have thought from the way they acted that there was a first-class war being carried on, even within the city limits. They went on about their usual affairs with the utmost serenity, stepping into a doorway when the first warning scream of a shell was heard, and then resuming their business after the third one had passed over. Whenever a shell struck a building, repairs were started almost before the smoke had cleared away—unless, of course, it happened to be during the *siesta* period.

On the second of May, LaCalle showed up at the hotel with a new Plymouth to haul me back to the field, and I was only too willing to get back into harness again. I figured that there was less risk in front line firing than there was in vacationing in the city of Madrid. On the way out to the field I asked him about Chang again, but he was still unable to supply any information.

When I arrived at Campo X, I discovered that my plane was still in the throes of its general overhaul. My mechanic, Chamorro, beamed proudly as he showed me a complete new set of cylinders and pistons which had already been mounted on the motor. The wings and fuselage had been re-covered and were glistening with new paint. When I finished my inspection I was beaming too, because it looked as though the plane was just as good as new. I didn't know, at the time, that I was never to have the pleasure of flying that particular plane again.

I did have the pleasure, however, of spending the rest of the day loafing around the count's place and resting up from the ordeal in Madrid. On the other hand, I had a rather bad quarter of an hour explaining certain things to María which she seemed to have heard from some of the squadron members who had seen me in action in various Madrid night clubs. She even had the names of some of the clubs and insinuated that when she had been living in Madrid they had had reputations which would embarrass her too much to mention. I hastened to explain that all that had changed since her departure from the city, and that they had become paragons of respectability, otherwise I would never have been seen there; that if I had happened to be in them with a girl, it was only because I was doing a favor for a friend; and finally that, anyway, the girl wasn't nearly as beautiful as she, María, was. Her eyes were beginning to flash dangerously until the final statement. As soon as I could get Justo and Magrinán off to the side I managed to persuade them to back up my story; which they did most convincingly, even going so far as to be intimately acquainted with the "friend" for whom I had been doing the favors. After that, my welcome in the sewing room was once more assured.

It was further assured by the fact that I had had the foresight to bring back some very high-grade American and English toilet soap. At that time toilet soap was very scarce all over the Guadalajara Valley. The only soap available was a rather crude type of homemade soap which, though suitable for washing clothes, was not considered by the young ladies as quite the thing for their complexions. Therefore, when I presented María and Cristina with a half-dozen bars of very elegant and loud-smelling soap they were ready to forgive me anything.

Chamorro came up to the sewing room the next morning and informed me that my plane was all ready for a test flight. I had already got into my parachute and was just getting ready to climb into the plane when a car came dashing up from Alcalá with the information that I was to be transferred to Kosokov's squadron, and that my plane should be turned over to some other pilot. José had decided that it would be better if Baumler and I, as the only two remaining Americans in the fighting-planes, were in the same squadron.

That afternoon Baumler came over in one of his squadron's cars and hauled me and my luggage over to the field used by Kosokov and his squadron. This particular field, Campo Soto, was located on what had formerly been the country estate of the Duke of Albuquerque. So I at least went up in the social world— moving from the estate of a former count to that of a former duke. We lived in the sumptuous, though ancient, principal building. Baumler and I lived in one of the former nursery rooms up on the second floor. At least we figured that it must have been one of the nursery rooms, because its walls were decorated with paintings of various and sundry fairy-tale characters which we still remembered from our misspent childhood days. As I already knew most of the pilots in the squadron, very few introductions were necessary, except to the group of *señoritas* who looked after the place in much the same manner that those at Azuqueca had done.

There were two extraordinary dogs with the squadron. The first one was the only shell-shocked dog I have ever seen. He was a big reddish St. Bernard, and he was absolutely unable to keep his mind concentrated on anything for more than a minute or so at a time. The first time I saw him he was sniffing and scratching at a plain old knothole in a large plank. Instinct told him, I suppose, that mice lived in holes, and he figured out that a hole therefore meant a mouse. He would vary this by dashing erratically over to the soft dirt on top of a newly constructed bomb shelter and digging frantically. That, I suppose, was because he had buried a bone somewhere and figured that it would be easier to look for it in the soft dirt than to do his searching elsewhere. I doubt, however, if he had ever been able to concentrate long enough on one task to bury a bone completely. His usual gait was exactly like that of a man suffering from locomotor ataxia and gave one the impression that he was always just on the verge of falling down through sheer clumsiness. He had been shell-shocked at Málaga when he was a puppy. He had been on the flying field there when it was shelled by Rebel ships. One of the mechanics had seen him running around among the shell bursts and had picked him up and taken him along in the last transport plane to leave the field. They had named the puppy *Metralla*, which means shrapnel.

The other was a fine German police dog called Tarzan, and was just as smart as Metralla was dumb. He was possibly the only bomber hound in the world. Baumler informed me—and I later verified it myself—that he invariably gave the first alarm when enemy bombers came over at night. For quite a while the Junkers had been in the habit of coming over either during, or shortly after, the evening meal. After they had been bombed a few times, the men noticed that Tarzan began to have mysterious spells of bark. As he had never barked before, they thought this was rather peculiar. Then they noticed that the night guards invariably fired off their bombardment alarm shots about fifteen or twenty seconds after the start of the barking.

After that there were no more surprise night bombardments. Whenever Tarzan sounded the alarm, all hands would lay down their knives and forks and wend their way, in a dignified manner, through the trees to the bomb shelter. Without such warning it was a matter of making a wild dash through the darkness with nothing except occasional bomb flashes as aids to navigation.

Believe me, whenever Kosokov's squadron moved to a different field, Tarzan went along. The most remarkable thing was that the dog never made a mistake. He could even tell the difference between the noises made by our own bombers and those made by enemy bombers, barking only at the latter.

CHAPTER XII

WORK AND PLAY—AND A SPY

On the morning of May fifth I made my first flight with my new squadron. We arose at 3:30 in the morning and took off before daylight. There were five of us, and we each had the usual four bombs apiece. We were supposed to go over behind the Guadalajara front and bomb some Fiats which had been seen by one of our observation planes the day before. First we flew over the field at Alcalá, where we met one of our Katiuskas which was supposed to lead us to the field in question. As it turned out, we had to find the field ourselves: the Katiuska pilot was evidently either rather green or had never flown on that front before, as he not only got lost himself but almost lost us, too. Fortunately, several of us knew that particular part of the country, so we managed to get ourselves and the Katiuska to the field in question.

But the Fiats weren't there—they had probably seen our observation plane and removed themselves to some other field. So we went to our secondary objective—a railroad station at a little town called Espinosa de Henares—and bombed a freight train which happened to be there at the time. The Katiuska and three of the other planes went wide of the target, but Baumler and I scored on the locomotive and the first of the freight cars. Then we came around and strafed it with our machine guns a couple of times. As the train was afire in two or three places when we left, we were able to go home feeling very well pleased with ourselves.

The plane I used in that flight was certainly a wreck. It had been assigned to me when I joined the new squadron and was much worse than my old plane had been before its overhaul. Its motor stopped four times before we got to the above-mentioned railroad station and five times on the way back to Campo Soto. So it was retired for an overhaul and I was promised a new one as soon as it could be obtained.

Baumler and I had been staying in the same room with two

Spanish pilots who followed the European custom of sleeping with the doors and windows hermetically sealed. The room had a wide, double door which opened on a large terrace built over the front veranda of the house, but every time we opened either it or the two windows the Spanish boys would manage to close them at some time during the night. We put up several kicks, but they did no good, so we decided to take matters into our own hands. We pushed both of our beds out on the terrace and announced our intention of sleeping out there. That maneuver completely baffled both the Spaniards and the Russians. The Spaniards, especially, were positive that the night air would kill us before daylight; they had never heard of such a thing.

Kosokov walked around on the terrace for about fifteen minutes, with a puzzled look on his face, before asking us how come? We explained that sleeping in a stuffy, airless room was bad for the health. He pondered this jewel of wisdom for a while and indicated that he thought it was a lot of bunk. However, the very progressive squadron doctor confirmed our statement, so that was all there was to it. It still remained a source of astonishment to our fellow pilots, though, when we continued to arise in the best of health every morning, in spite of sleeping out in the open air.

We soon had our terrace living quarters in fine shape. The personnel officer had it scrubbed the day after we moved out there, and it was swept every morning. We had a table, several chairs, glasses, pitchers and even a couple of full siphon bottles on hand at all times. We were both on excellent terms with the house *señoritas* by that time, so they always kept the terrace spick and span. The secret of our pull with them was that I had brought the soap system along with me. We made it a habit to bring perfumed toilet soap back to them whenever we went in to Madrid. An occasional bar of it worked wonders.

New planes were very scarce at that time, so I soon learned that I would have to use the old one—after they had put in a new motor—one of the new Russian Cyclone motors. Our old motors had all been Wright Cyclones built in Paterson, New Jersey; but the new ones had actually been built in Russia. They were exactly like the Wrights except that they had about fifty more

146

horsepower, and this was given to them by a new type of carburettor which the Russians had developed for that particular engine.

The reason for my sudden interest in engines was that rumors had been circulating around that we were to fly up to Santander, on the northern coast of Spain. The trip would involve flying over a considerable amount of enemy territory, so we wanted to be sure that our motors were in perfect condition before the start. This rumor was confirmed by the arrival of a Spanish pilot named Jover, who had been sent to lead our planes to Santander.

On one of these days of leisure I talked Kosokov into letting me have a car for the trip over to Campo X to visit the old squadron, but when I arrived there I found that Jiménez had just started out for Santander that morning. Later we learned that they had got lost and landed somewhere in France, and had almost been interned by the international non-intervention patrol members up there. When I found that they had already gone, I went over to Azuqueca and visited around with a few of the ground crew members in the *casa de mecánicos* and then had dinner at the pilots' house. There I noticed Chang's personal effects were still in our old room, but no one had heard anything about him since he left. After dinner I visited María and Cristina out at the field house, and then went in to Madrid for a bath. When I returned to Campo Soto that evening I found that my plane's overhaul had been completed and that it had been test-hopped by Jover, the new pilot. I didn't like that very much, as I always like to test my own planes; but I did have time enough left to go over and have the motor revved up on the ground. Its performance was excellent; it would turn up more than 1600 revolutions per minute on the ground, whereas my old plane could just barely turn up 1500.

On May tenth I made my first reconnaissance flight in a long time. As it was over territory that I had never flown over before, it was fairly interesting. It was to the westward of the Sierra Guadarrama, the highest mountain range in Spain. That morning I took off with two other pilots and headed north along the Madrid-Burgos highway. After we crossed the mountains, we noticed a convoy of about fifteen enemy trucks filing down the road on the other side. That was the only sign of enemy activity that we saw. After we finished our observations, mostly over and around the city of Segovia, we returned to that road and went into action.

We went down on the trucks in formation the first time, all machine guns working, to break up their formation. That so rattled the idiots that they made a very grave blunder; instead of stopping at once, they stepped on their accelerators. We then came around and went down the road after them, flying one after the other. That time we really caught them square. Every time we pulled up and around we could see trucks either burning, rolling down the mountain side, or running into each other. I remember that all the time we were engaged in this harmless pastime I was humming *She'll Be Coming Round the Mountain* in synchronization with the wide-open roar of my new motor. When we tired of that sport we went back over the mountains and reported the results of the trip to Kosokov at Campo Soto.

The following day Madrid citizens got their first sight of Government planes in action since our bombing activities of a month before. Baumler and I and a young Spanish pilot named Bastido were sent to try to locate a new artillery battery which had opened up on Madrid a few days before. Its general direction was known, but its exact location was not. So we went up just before the time when it usually opened up. And the enemy anti-aircraft gunners came closer to getting us that day than they had ever come before.

When we first arrived over the city we cruised above the suspected area at an altitude of 6000 feet and couldn't see a thing. There wasn't a sign of any anti-aircraft fire; I suppose they were calculating our altitude and speed and getting their sights all set. We circled around over the city and came back at an altitude of about 3000 feet. Just as we got back over enemy territory again, they opened up with everything they had. About sixteen greasy black bursts blossomed out just behind our formation. They were so close that we could hear them exploding, even above the roar of our motors.

We immediately went into a sharp left dive and then, with the extra speed gathered by that maneuver, proceeded to give the spectators a display of aerial acrobatics in formation. Bastido, however, who was rather inexperienced, got lost on one of our turns and almost got shot for his mistake. He could hardly be blamed for getting lost, though, because we were winding and twisting around in all directions. It seemed that every time we finally got over our own territory again we could look back and see our exact course traced out by the gradually disappearing black puffs, greatly resembling a string of carelessly thrown beads. But we still hadn't been able to spot the offending battery.

We got back in formation over the bull ring and went back for another try. We figured that the battery had a camouflaging cover on it, so this time we dived right down toward the assigned area and managed to see flashes coming out from under a darkish-looking patch on the ground. We carefully marked the location of this patch on our maps and, when we returned to the field, reported this information to Kosokov. That night, just after leaving the field, we had the satisfaction of hearing that the offending battery had been silenced.

That field of ours at Campo Soto was very interesting. It had been the first one used by the Russians when they surprised the Fascists with their new fighting-planes. It had been in constant use ever since that time, but had never been discovered by the enemy. The reason for this was that it was very well camouflaged, and the planes could be completely concealed from aerial observation when they were on the ground.

The field itself was so narrow that it could only be landed on from two directions—east and west. It had a false road winding across it and two or three false ditches. Its southern boundary was marked by a real creek, and just south of this creek was the duke's grove of trees, in the middle of which was our group of buildings. There were two wide, camouflaged bridges across the creek, and as soon as the planes landed they were taxied across these bridges and parked under the large oak trees. The Fascists knew there was a field in that vicinity, but they never were able to get its exact location. This field was the closest one to Madrid that we had—only four or five minutes away by air—so it was almost invaluable.

Baumler and I used the southernmost of the two bridges and

parked our planes around the edges of a little glade bounded on three sides by trees and on the fourth by the creek. We had very little to do while we were there, and were very fortunate in having such comfortable surroundings in which to do our loafing. It was so long since I had slept under a real tree that it was almost like being back in the timber country of good old Arkansas County.

The creek had a sandy bottom and was more or less dried up at that time. In the occasional pools, however, we were able to find snakes and fish to study in our spare time. Since the snakes were a small, harmless variety of water snake, we usually took one or two back to the house with us with which to scare the girls—also some of the boys. I took one of them up to our terrace one afternoon and, after scaring the girls with it, threw the thing out in the garden. Then, when they rather timidly returned, I assured them that I had placed it in the room where Kosokov and two or three other Russians were living at the time. This information they conveyed to Kosokov, and although he and his compatriots asserted that it made no difference to them, we noticed that all of them except Kosokov came out on our terrace that night to sleep, remarking that it was too hot in their room.

There was also a family of large green lizards living under an old log about fifty feet in front of Baumler's plane. We passed many an hour either observing their actions or trying to catch them. They were lightning fast, so that it was almost impossible to catch them by surprise. One of them, known as Oscar, had a habit of crawling under a large piece of corrugated iron. It was about four feet square and was lying on the ground about six feet from one end of the log and eventually proved to be Oscar's undoing. One of our mechanics lifted up the slab while Baumler and I stood by, and when Oscar made his usual dash for the log, I was able to stun him with a piece of bomb crate. Oscar was about fifteen inches long, with a thick, heavy body, and was equipped with a vicious looking set of teeth. He came to in about ten minutes and we released him. The next day he was back under the plate again, as well as ever. The Spanish boys said they were poisonous, but I don't think that they knew what they were talking about.

On the thirteenth of May we made a curious flight which had us all baffled until its purpose was explained later. The entire squadron took off and made three round-trip flights around a course marked by our field, Madrid, Alcalá and Guadalajara. The entire affair took us one hour and fifty minutes. When we landed we found that the flight had been made to see if the planes carried enough fuel for the trip to Santander. What Baumler and I couldn't see was why they hadn't sent just one or two planes to make the test instead of sending the whole squadron. It seemed to us that it was a useless waste of gasoline.

The following day they piled all the pilots into squadron cars and drove us over to look at the field from which we were to leave. It was a way up on the side of the *sierra*, right by the side of the lake which supplied Madrid with drinking water. Although the field was smooth enough, it was one of the smallest I had seen up to that time. It was about three miles from the little village of Manzanares de la Sierra.

That night I found that my plane's motor was too good. Jover, who was to lead the flight, decided that he wanted it. That was the starting point for a most vituperative argument, with practically everyone on my side. However, Kosokov drew me off to one side and told me that if I let Jover have my plane, I could use his (Kosokov's) plane. As he flew one of the best all-round fighting-planes we had, I immediately agreed. When I went back into the fray and called off my backers-up, Jover became so suspicious of my motives that I was afraid, for a minute, that he was going to change his mind about wanting my plane.

Jover wasn't such a bad fellow to get along with except that, like Jiménez, he didn't seem to have the ability of a natural leader. He was chosen to lead the flight to Santander because he had flown up there quite a bit at the start of the war. He had shot down a couple of planes up there before getting shot down himself. In the crash he was rather badly burned and had spent several months in the hospital recovering. So he couldn't be blamed too much for wanting to be sure that the next plane he flew wouldn't be forced to make a crash landing. Such tactics are not wise, however; pilots are very touchy about their planes, especially in wartime.

As it turned out, it didn't make any difference, anyway; for the following day we received word that no Russian or American pilots were to make the trip. The Government didn't want to take the chance of having any foreigners fall into the enemy's hands on account of motor trouble. So all of the Spanish pilots took off and, as far as we could find out, left for Santander the next day.

On the afternoon of the day they left, Baumler and the Russian went into Madrid to see Charlie Chaplin, but as I had already seen the show I stayed at the field. I spent most of the afternoon walking through the woods along the banks of the Manzanares River, looking for a boat. My search was unsuccessful, but I did manage to go swimming for a while. The water was from the melting snow of the nearby mountains, a little too cold for comfort.

After my swim I returned to the house and amused the girls by starting a couple of fights between the shell-shocked Metralla and a nondescript police dog whom Baumler and I had named Sneerpuss. He received this nickname because at some time in his fighting career he had received a scar on one side of his mouth, which gave one the impression that he was always sneering. This effect was enhanced by the fact that the hackles on the back of his neck were standing straight on end at all times.

In these fights Metralla showed his shell-shocked condition most unmistakably. As long as I kept shouting encouragement, he would keep on fighting viciously and effectively; but within a few seconds after I stopped, he would lose interest in the fight and start scratching at the ground or sniffing at a tree-hollow, while Sneerpuss would be getting in his best work—with no visible effect upon Metralla's tranquility. He had so much fur that even a wolf-like police dog couldn't hurt him.

We made no more flights for at least two weeks after the departure of Jover and his boys. We spent our spare time either swimming, walking through the woods, starting dogfights, or courting the *señoritas*. Baumler and I also spent quite a bit of time trying to persuade Kosokov (whom we had nicknamed "the Old Stud") that we should be transferred to the low-winged monoplane fighters. On the nineteenth we got a car and went over to visit friends at Alcalá and Azuqueca. At Alcalá we met the regional commander, my old friend José, and he told us that we were going to be transferred to the monoplanes, if we could fly them. Needless to say, we were overjoyed.

We didn't realize until later how great an honor was being conferred upon us. Before this time only Russians had been allowed to fly the low-wingers in Spain, and we were the first non-Russians to be invited to join one of their squadrons. Even LaCalle had been unable to try one of them out. We figured that we were invited to join because of the fact that our flying records were pretty good. Baumler had cracked up one plane, but it had not been his fault, so it didn't count.

We wound up our trip by going over to Campo X for dinner. There we found a squadron of biplanes—piloted by Russians. Most of them were new pilots, but there were two or three of the old boys we had known before. They gave us the interesting information that all the old monoplane pilots were to be relieved by new ones in the near future. While at the field I also managed to see my old girl friend, María. Her sister, Cristina, had been sent to the new field at Manzanares de la Sierra. They were still without any news about Chang.

On the twenty-first Baumler and I got permission from the Old Stud to go to Valencia for three days, so we loaded up our car—a new V-8—and dashed over to Alcalá to get our official permits from the *Jefe de Campo* (Chief of the Field). As soon as we got the necessary permits we started out for Valencia. We wanted to be sure that we got away before they changed their minds.

That was one of the most interesting drives I have ever taken. We had a Spanish chauffeur along, so both of us had plenty of time to look at the scenery along our route. And there was certainly plenty of it; practically every hill had either an old castle or an old Roman watchtower on top of it. Our only gripe was that we didn't have time to investigate the ruins. The old Roman watchtowers (our chauffeur thought they were brick kilns) are square stone structures about thirty feet square and fifty feet high. They are of such solid construction that most of them are in a perfect state of preservation. Even the base of the very excellent road we were traveling was laid by the Romans.

Possibly the most beautiful spot on the entire road is where it crosses the Cabriel River. The river bed is about 2500 feet below the surrounding plain, so that the road on each side of the gorge has to make at least ten complete S-turns before it gets down to the river itself. And the entire road can be seen from any of the S-turn shoulders.

We arrived in Valencia about 8:30 that night and went to the Hotel Inglés. There we ran into Major LaCalle and Barca, Jim's former mechanic. LaCalle was just on the verge of leaving for Russia, so when he invited us to have dinner with him that night we accepted with pleasure. As there were no rooms available at either the Hotel Inglés or the Hotel Regina, we went over to the Officers' Pavilion and got a couple of rooms there. After getting our luggage stowed away and washing up, we returned to the Hotel Inglés and had dinner with LaCalle. We asked him about Chang; he could not give us any information but said they might know something about him up at the Air Ministry.

The next day we went up to the Air Ministry to see if we had any mail, which we did. There we met an old friend, the Spanish-English interpreter, Pliny. He managed to get off, so we went out to the port and tried to go aboard various and sundry freighters at the piers, but with no success. We had passes from the Ministry of Maritime Affairs, but it seemed that they were valid only for passage through the port gates.

That afternoon we managed to get a double room at the Hotel Inglés and moved into it at once. We then hung around the lobby for a while waiting for Pliny; and while so occupied we met a few more Americans—Bob Minor, James Hawthorne and other assorted writers and newspaper men. We wound up the day by having dinner with Pliny; that is, we thought we had wound it up. The outskirts of the city were bombarded at about 2 o'clock in the morning, and the management woke us up to tell us about it. We informed the management that we were quite accustomed to being bombed at night and asked them, please, to mind their own damned business. It seemed that the citizens of Valencia weren't accustomed, at that time, to night bombardments. When the city was bombarded again the next night, the management didn't tell us about it till the next morning. This time a large apartment house quite close to the Inglés was struck. We watched them search the débris for bodies—and finding portions of them. Many of the civilians were standing around watching the operations, too. Once, when the shattered remains of a small child were brought up, a few of them showed signs of emotion, but the majority of them never so much as moved a muscle of their faces. It seems that human beings can become accustomed to anything. I suppose that, if we ever go into a war on a large scale, we may expect more or less of the same thing. I can almost see the crowds standing around watching the Little Rock Fire Department dig bodies out of the Albert Pike or the Ben McGhee hotels—though why any enemy with good sense would want to bomb Little Rock I couldn't say—and philosophically discussing the condition of the remains.

Just before leaving time the next morning Pliny came rushing up with last minute permission to go to Madrid with us. So we went over to his quarters and loaded his duffle aboard, too. The car was pretty well overloaded, so we weren't at all surprised at having two blowouts on the way back. We managed to get to Campo Soto all right, however, and then we let Pliny have the car for the trip in to Madrid.

On the twenty-sixth of May, Baumler and I found out—accidentally—the truth about Chang's mysterious disappearance some two months before. We happened to be talking to Kosokov about spies, and one of us asked him if he thought there were any in the Government's aviation branch. He said that there certainly were some, and went on to say that only a few weeks before they had caught up with one in LaCalle's squadron. At that, both of us pricked up our ears and pressed him for further details. He had evidently let this information slip out without thinking, because he didn't seem to care very much about saying any more on the subject. However, we both went to work on him and managed to worm enough information out of him to make it quite evident that Chang was the one he referred to.

He said that the one they caught was a very short fellow, and that he could speak Spanish, English, Japanese and Russian. We both knew that Chang could speak the first three languages but we hadn't known that he could also speak Russian. That left no doubt at all that it had been Chang. Kosokov went on to say that he had been caught spying against the Russian aviation units for the Japanese Government. He assured us that Chang had not been spying against the Spanish Government for Franco. However, when we asked him what they had done with Chang, he pointed an imaginary pistol at his head and said, "*fusilado*." When we rather foolishly asked him if Chang was dead, he elaborated with "*Chang—no hay más*" (there is no longer any Chang).

It was quite a shock to discover that a man with whom I had lived and flown for over two months had been a spy all that time. He had even used my fountain pen in doing all his writing, so I suppose that I was an unwitting accessory to the fact. He had done so much writing that I used to let him keep it all the time, only getting it from him to write my very occasional letters. He had even had it with him when he left, making it necessary for me to do all my subsequent writing with a pencil.

As soon as we found this out, it cleared up a lot of things that had seemed a little strange. I remembered that most of Chang's letter writing had been to a "sister" in Tokyo, Japan. Then we both remembered LaCalle's evasiveness when we questioned him as to Chang's whereabouts; when he talked to us, denying any knowledge of Chang, he hadn't gestured with his hands. And one of LaCalle's characteristics was that whenever he was telling a damned lie his hands remained idle. At all other times he used violent gestures. We also thought it rather strange that a squadron commander should be kept in ignorance as to the whereabouts of one of his men. We finally decided that LaCalle had known the truth all along but didn't want to tell us because he knew that we had considered Chang our friend.

The chief mechanic at Campo Soto was a huge Russian known as Basilio. He was an excellent guitar player and also had a fine baritone singing voice. As I had been getting in a little accordion practice, we were able to give several concerts during this period of inactivity. Neither of us knew any of the other's native songs, so we had to play Spanish songs which we had picked up here and there. We achieved our best harmony on *La Paloma* and *Cielito Lindo*. The trouble with the latter song was that it was rather popular in Spain, and our audience would usually drown out our most strenuous efforts whenever we tried to play it. Our best concerts were given in the bomb shelter during night bombardment alarms. The bomb shelter had certain resonant acoustical properties that gave our respective instruments tonal qualities which they were never able to achieve above ground— the sort of rolling resonance you get when you shout into an empty rain barrel or an abandoned well.

CHAPTER XIII

THRILLS IN A MONOPLANE

Baumler and I were booked for a trip to Tembleque, about 200 miles south of Madrid, so one day we packed up all our duffle and drove over to Alcalá. As usual, though, things were balled up. José told us that we were not to go to Tembleque after all, but would go into monoplanes as soon as possible. He also informed us that, if one of the Spanish pilots failed to make his appearance, one of us would have to ferry a plane up to Santander and then return in commercial planes by way of France. So once more we hauled our luggage back to Campo Soto, where we settled down for another period of loafing.

The next morning, however, the Spanish pilot showed up, so we were both sent over to the monoplane field at Alcalá, where we were formally introduced to the members of the squadron stationed there. They had all been in Spain long enough to be able to speak fairly good Spanish, so we got along fine. After our introduction we were each assigned to an instructor and then spent the remainder of the day examining the monoplanes. They had a plane blocked up on high sawhorses and made us practise raising and lowering the wheels several times apiece. The operation of the landing gear was very simple, but it seemed that new monoplane pilots had a habit of forgetting to lower their wheels when coming in for their first landings.

After thoroughly examining the planes, we spent our time getting acquainted with our new squadron mates. We soon had nicknames for most of them which we used when talking between ourselves. The squadron commander was a darkish little Russian named Ukov. My instructor was a comparatively small fellow named Lockiev. He had a rather vacant look, so we promptly nicknamed him "Goofy." Baumler's instructor was a tall fellow with a long, disgusted-looking face and a mouthful of gold teeth; he drew the name of "Sourpuss". They were both fine fellows, though, and we later became very good friends. The rest of the Russians were, almost without exception, huge blond specimens.

On the thirtieth of May we made our first flights in the famous monoplanes, each of us making several take-offs and landings. Baumler made the first flight, and when he finished I went up in the same plane. They were certainly wonderful planes; even that old training crate would make more than 250 miles on the straightaway. What they would make in a dive I never found out; their air-speed meters didn't go up as high as that. These planes were nothing more than a development of our own U.S. Army P-26, the principal developments being the retractable landing gear and the more powerful motor. Their motors were Russian cyclones of considerably more horsepower than the biplane motors. Their armament consisted of two automatic machine guns mounted out on the wings. They fired—outside of the propeller radius—at the unbelievable rate of 1800 bullets per minute, thereby giving a total volume of fire, with both guns, of 3600 bullets per minute.

The following day we each made a short flight for the purpose of getting the feel of our planes. On this occasion I made the first flight—after a ten-minute lecture from Goofy about the danger of forgetting to lower landing gear after acrobatic flights. On this flight I discovered that those planes had to be handled very gently. Twice, when I tried to use my usual biplane tactics, my plane promptly went into a right spin. Most of the controlling had to be done with ailerons and flippers; very little or no rudder being required, even in steep banks.

Just after I landed from this first flight we received a call to protect a squadron of Rasantes which was going over the Sierra to bomb the enemy trenches just outside of Segovia. I had evidently finished my training course, because I was given a plane and told to stand by to take off with the rest of the squadron. As Baumler hadn't had his acrobatics yet, I had the honor of being the first non-Russian to fly one of the monoplanes across the lines. I was assigned to fly the No. 4 position in Goofy's patrol, so he spent the remaining few minutes warning me again about landing with my wheels up. Then, when the Rasantes appeared over the field, we climbed up into position above them.

Segovia is about 45 miles north-west of Alcalá. To get there we had to fly over the highest part of the Sierra Guadarrama. As we usually flew about 3000 feet higher than the Rasantes, we were up in rather chilly atmosphere most of the time. Our planes were so much faster than the bombers that we were continually making huge S-turns over them. This first flight was rather uneventful; the Rasantes went through a little anti-aircraft fire, but we weren't bothered at all.

I was one of the last to land when we returned to Alcalá and as I came in I saw a plane lying flat on its belly out in the middle of the field. As I taxied in to my parking position I wondered what could have happened. My bewilderment was further increased when my mechanic, Pedro, informed me that it was Goofy's plane. Then, when I motored in to the operations office, Baumler told me that Goofy had landed with his wheels up. After all his lectures to me on the subject!

Baumler was certainly relieved to find that it hadn't been I who made the blunder. He said that when the plane landed with its wheels up every one of the ground force immediately murmured, "*el americano*". They all assumed that I was the culprit. When Baumler discovered the truth, he almost got both of us into trouble by openly gloating over the calamity howlers. Poor old Goofy had the most sheepish look on his face that I have ever seen. His feelings weren't at all elevated when I asked him in a stage whisper if he had landed that way just to show me how to do it.

Later that afternoon Baumler made his acrobatics flight, doing a much better job of it than I had done; so we were both full-fledged members of the squadron. We then hung around the field for the remainder of the day, but were not called upon to make any more flights. So we went in to the pilots' house in Alcalá and turned in for the night.

The following day, June first, we really went to work on Segovia in earnest, making three trips over the Sierra with our Rasantes. On our first trip we waited until the Rasantes finished their work and then went over back of Segovia and machine-gunned some enemy trucks which were hidden in a little grove of trees. On the other two trips we merely flew protection while the

Rasantes did their stuff; and they really did it. There were about fifteen of them, and each time they bombed and machine-gunned the enemy trenches from the east to the south of the city. As far as we could see, all their bombs landed either in or between the fascist primary and secondary trenches.

Late that afternoon General Douglas flew in from Albacete in a biplane fighter. After congratulating Baumler and me on our excellent showing, he harangued the Russian pilots for a while in Russian. As far as we could gather, he was giving them the latest news from Russia, and from the expressions on their faces it must have been pretty good news.

The next day was very busy and eventful. We made four flights. Our first flight was the usual one with Rasantes and everything came off as per schedule. On our second flight we had a two-rocket alarm, but when we arrived at Segovia we could see nothing. On our third flight, with Rasantes, we ran into our first opposition. We had a twenty-minute dogfight with a couple of squadrons of Fiats. The first of them came right out of the sun at our patrol; and we didn't even see them until they were going by. After that we had a pretty warm time of it. I fired at several of them but, still being unaccustomed to the new-style machine guns, I don't believe that I hit any of them. However, as the squadron got credit for three Fiats, we didn't do badly; we didn't lose any planes at all.

Our last flight of the day was the best of all. The enemy was lying in ambush for us. We went over with our usual convoy of Rasantes, and about fifty assorted Heinkels and Fiats came down on top of us from out of the sun, which at that time was low in the west. The atmosphere was very hazy, with a high layer of cumulus clouds, and the sun's rays coming through in places made visibility extremely poor. Before we knew it we were all balled up in the biggest dogfight we were to have on that front. I had to fire at seven or eight of them before I managed to finish one of them off.

I looked down and saw a Fiat fighter right behind one of our biplanes. I threw my plane into a right half-roll and was down behind the poor Fiat before he even knew it. My first burst of bullets set fire to his motor and my last got the pilot as he stood up and started to jump. I didn't intend to shoot the pilot before he jumped, but I was still a little unused to my new plane and couldn't seem to get out of gear once I started firing. So there was nothing to do about it but hope that it might have been one of Mussolini's relatives. There was no chance of that, though, as Il Duce knew better than to send any of them out in fighting-planes. One of his brave boys did fly a bombing plane over Mallorca and bomb the open city of Valencia, but he was accompanied by an experienced bombardment pilot.

Just after this incident I noticed that our last patrol of Rasantes was under fire, so I and two or three others went over and chased the attackers away. Before we could get there, though, they had managed to set fire to one of the Rasantes. An explosive bullet must have struck its gas tank, because it burst into flames all at once. We saw the pilot and the gunner take to their parachutes and, as they were almost directly over no-man's land, we wondered how they were going to make out.

There were no more planes in the sky now except our own. After cruising around for about fifteen minutes longer, just to make that fact evident to the enemy ground troops, we went back to the home field. There I had the first and only landing accident of my entire piloting career. There was a strong, gusty crosswind blowing and just when I had completed about two thirds of my landing roll, a gust hit the plane. It whirled around in a fast right ground loop, causing the left wheel to collapse, which threw the plane over on its left wing.

As soon as that happened the Tee was changed and the rest of the planes came in safely, angling across the field. All that my plane needed to put it back into service was a new left wing. Even the left wheel was undamaged. One of the supporting wire cables had broken, and that was easily replaced.

When Baumler landed, he taxied in to the operations office instead of going to his assigned parking position on the field. The tail of his plane had been struck by two or three explosive bullets and a large fragment of shrapnel had struck each of his shoulders. He would probably have been seriously wounded if the fragments had not passed through the steel seat back and his parachute straps before getting to him. It seemed that he had got behind a Fiat and, while he was shooting at it, a Heinkel had come down behind him. Anyway, he was soon patched up and as well as ever.

That night we found out the results of the day's work. The enemy had lost nine Heinkels and Fiats, and we had lost one Rasante, one biplane and one monoplane. The Rasante was the one we had seen go down in flames. The biplane was piloted by the Russian commander of a new biplane squadron which had just come up to that front the day before. The monoplane was from some other squadron and we never did find out who was piloting it. That night, though, we heard that the Rasante had been piloted by an American! This new really astounded Baumler and me. We had been under the impression that we were the last American pilots over there. A little further inquiry brought out the fact that it was Finnick, whom we had last seen at the flying field at Manises, just outside of Valencia. As far as we could find out, he had landed in our lines and was burned or wounded, but not in any immediate danger.

The following day, both of our planes being under repair, we took a run to Madrid. We visited the Air Ministry and spent the remainder of the day shopping around for clothes, soap and English books. Our favorite bootlegger had also saved out two bottles of Scotch whisky which he sold to us at an exorbitant price. When we finally arrived at the Hotel Florida we ran into our old friends from the Lincoln Brigade, so we all went up to one of their rooms and reminisced over the Scotch. We then wound the day up by taking hot baths and dashing back to Alcalá.

On June fourth we made only one flight over the Sierra to Segovia, and that was a routine patrol flight. Just as we came around a large bank of clouds, we saw a single Fiat coming out from under another cloud bank. He was about 1500 feet below us—evidently out scouting—and never did see our planes. Little Ukov, the squadron commander, signaled to the rest of us to stay up where we were, and then went into a half-roll and pulled back on his stick. He fell down on the unfortunate Fiat like a falcon. He fired two or three short bursts and then pulled back up into formation—he knew he had got his man. The Fiat skidded up into a mushy stall and then went into a spin, crashing into the side of the mountain down below. The pilot must have been killed, because he had not taken to his parachute, although he had plenty of time.

Baumler and I were having a fine time with our Victrola. The clerk in Valencia had accidentally picked out some of the best records we had ever heard. Our favorite was a large record with selections from the Italian opera *Rigoletto* on both sides. Every time we came in from a flight we would play that record at least once. It seemed to have a soothing influence on our nerves.

From the fifth to the ninth of June we made no flights at all. Our squadron was divided into two groups, half of us being on duty from 4:30 in the morning to 1 o'clock in the afternoon, and the other half being on duty from that time until about 8 at night. This was quite a relief after our all-day tours of duty, and we spent many pleasant hours looking over the city of Alcalá or lying around the pilots' house. Cervantes, the author of *Don Quixote*, had lived in a house only a half-block away from our house. It is a sort of museum now and has been restored to its original condition by the Government.

On the tenth we had a double-rocket alarm and dashed over to the Guadalajara front, but saw nothing. That afternoon we were informed that we were to get ready to go up to the Aragon front the next day. As we had just found out where Finnick was hospitalized, we got permission to go over and visit him. We brought along cigarettes, books, Victrola and anything else we could think of that he might be able to use.

He was in hospital only about 35 miles from Alcalá, so it took us only an hour to get there. We found poor Finnick with one leg in a cast and various face and body burns still in the process of healing. He was very pleased to see us and told us all about what had happened when he was shot down.

He hadn't even been aware of the fact that he was being attacked until his gas tank burst into flames. The flames had spread so rapidly that he and his gunner had both been badly burned before they could get clear of the plane. Finnick's burns were the worst, because he had been closer to the gas tank. After his parachute opened he noticed that his clothes were afire and, worst of all, one of his parachute straps was smoldering. The latter fire, however, went out of its own accord, and he was able to turn his entire attention to beating out the fire in his clothes.

Then, when he neared the ground, his parachute hung up in the branches of a large tree and left him dangling about twenty feet from the ground, with shells and bullets whistling all around. So he started yanking at the parachute straps. The parachute came loose suddenly, and in the twenty-foot drop to the ground his left leg was broken; and he still didn't know whether he was in enemy territory or his own.

Shortly after his fall he heard shouting and men crashing through the underbrush. Not knowing who they were, he pulled out his pistol and crawled behind the tree just as a squad of militiamen burst out of the shrubbery. He recognized the red star emblem of the Government forces on their caps and knew he was in our territory. He therefore dropped his pistol and called out to them. But when they heard his broken Spanish they immediately concluded that he was either a German or an Italian. They were just about to shoot him when an English-speaking lieutenant came along and saved him. When the lieutenant found out that Finnick was an American, he had him carried to the nearest emergency hospital.

Later I met the English-speaking lieutenant who had saved Finnick's life, but that is another story. Before we left, Finnick told us that his leg was going to have to be re-broken and reset, as it had been improperly set in the front line emergency hospital. We cheered him up as best we could, and then went back to Alcalá to get ready for our trip up into north-east Spain.

On the eleventh we made our first flight into Catalonian territory. We made it in two jumps, the first one from Alcalá to Liria, about nine miles from Valencia, and the second from Liria to a field near the little village of Barbastro. On the trip to Liria, Ukov was leading our squadron, while Goofy, who had been promoted, was leading another group of six planes. When we landed at Liria there wasn't a sign of Goofy and his six planes. Finally, a phone call came in from Valencia informing us that six of our planes had missed Liria and landed at Manises, but that they were on their way over. When they appeared over the field and came in, one by one, we saw an excellent demonstration of discipline—something we never thought existed in Russian squadrons.

We were all sitting on the shady side of a long adobe building when Goofy came walking in with a very sheepish grin on his face. We had the commanding officer of all our various squadrons with us, and he got up on his feet when Goofy came up. He asked some question—in Russian—and Goofy made the mistake of trying to laugh it off. Then he snapped out an order which brought Goofy up standing. He walked over directly in front of the commanding officer, clicked his heels together and started off in official Russian military phraseology. Soon we could see that Goofy's story wasn't going over very well, because the cloud on the major's face kept getting darker. At each ominous "yes" from his superior, Goofy would deflate a little more, until he finally looked only about half as big as he had looked at the beginning of his explanation. Finally, Baumler and I couldn't stand watching the slaughter any longer, so we walked around the corner of the building. All the Russian pilots, however, stayed there to see the show. In the end, Goofy must have managed to square himself, because when we took off for Castejón he was still in command of his six planes.

The flight to Barbastro was one of the most interesting cross-country flights we ever had in Spain. We flew up the coast until we reached the mouth of the Ebro River, followed it to the mouth of the Río Chico, and then followed the Chico up to Barbastro. Thus in this one flight we saw practically every type of scenery to be seen in Spain. The Mediterranean, the coastal plains, the river valleys, the hill country and finally, when we arrived over Barbastro, we could see the Pyrenees off to the northward.

Our field there was in good shape except that it had tall weeds on part of it. It was both big enough and smooth enough to suit our monoplanes, so we overlooked the weeds. It was about 18 miles due east of Huesca, our immediate objective, putting us within easy striking distance of that city. The situation at Huesca was about the same as it had been at Teruel when we first arrived at that front. It was occupied by the Rebels, but our troops were on three sides of it, leaving a bottleneck leading out to the westward along the railroad and the highway to Zaragoza. Our mission was to assist our ground troops in cutting this bottleneck and isolating the city from the remainder of Franco's territory.

We went into Barbastro that night and found our quarters were on the third floor of a three-story building. That would have been perfectly all right, but there was a stable full of mules and donkeys down on the ground floor, so we put up an immediate protest. We figured out that there was a little too much local atmosphere to suit us. It was finally decided that we would use that third floor as our dining hall—it could be ventilated well enough for that purpose—and would do our sleeping in another building which was not quite so odorous. We later noticed that quite a few of the houses in Barbastro had stables on the ground floor, so we inferred that it was merely an old Catalonian custom.

All our kicking was done to the political commissars assigned to our squadron. As we had two squadrons of monoplanes, we had two commissars to do our kicking to. One of them, a Russian, was evidently a fairly big shot in the Russian political organization in Spain, as he could really get things done when he wanted to. Baumler and I called him "the Powerhouse". The other one, also a Russian, was a very young fellow who was evidently just learning the commissar business, so he drew the nickname of "the Assistant Powerhouse". "The Powerhouse" was the one who got us into our new sleeping quarters in such short order.

Except Baumler and me, all the other pilots in the squadrons were Russians. All the plane mechanics were Spaniards under the general directorship of two Russian mechanics who acted as technical advisers. One of them was a huge pock-marked fellow named Gregoric and the other was a young chap who was somewhat of a dandy and was dubbed "Smoothie" the first time we set eyes on him. Gregoric handled all details connected with the motors, while "Smoothie" was the expert on fuselages, wings and tail assemblies.

On the twelfth we had our first look at the city of Huesca, making three trips up to the bottleneck with our bombing planes. Our first two trips were with Rasantes and our last one was with both Rasantes and Katiuskas. All the bombardments were very good, especially that of the Katiuskas on the last flight. They dropped some very heavy bombs along the enemy first-line trenches to the south of the bottleneck, evidently destroying a considerable number of parapets. We didn't see a sign of any enemy fight planes, however, so we considered the day more or less of a failure.

On Sunday we made no flights at all, apparently because the Aragonians are very religious and didn't want to interfere with any church-going inclinations the Fascists around Huesca might have. The other squadrons, though, made a routine patrol flight and had to drive off a few Fiats who were trying to strafe our trenches. The Fiats received a good peppering, but none of them were seen to strike the ground.

Our first flight the next day was in cooperation with a squadron of our Katiuskas. First we went up to the front and started strafing the enemy trenches to the east and south of Huesca. While we were doing that, the Katiuskas were sneaking around to the north of the city. They bombed the stuffing out of a little town called Ayerbe, about twelve miles west of Huesca, and managed to set something afire which was still burning furiously when we left the scene. As soon as the Katiuskas finished their bombing, we climbed up to protect them while they made their way back across the lines. There was no need of it, however, as there wasn't a sign of any enemy fighting-planes. Ayerbe was at an important highway and railroad junction, so no doubt the stuff we saw burning was gasoline or munitions.

Our second flight was even more interesting than the first. Two squadrons of our biplanes from another field had gone up to the front to engage in a little dive-bombing and had been attacked by about sixty Heinkels and Fiats. We got there just in time to save their hides. They were fighting all over the sky back of Huesca, but after we jumped into the conflict with our monoplanes it soon ended—we caught the poor fellows completely by surprise. However, it was certainly hot while it lasted, there being well over a hundred planes engaged in the conflict. Every way I turned there seemed to be at least one or two possible targets in sight. I fired at eight or ten of them, but was entirely too busy to take time out to see whether any of them hit the ground. Anyway, within twenty minutes after we arrived on the scene there wasn't an enemy plane in the sky. That night at dinner we got the results of the fight from the front line observers. The Fascists had lost fourteen assorted Heinkels and Fiats, while our side had lost three biplanes. On the strength of this good news we were even able to talk "The Powerhouse" into supplying an extra case of champagne for the celebration.

The following day we escorted a squadron of Rasantes over and beyond Huesca—where they did an excellent job of bombing the trenches in the bottleneck. There were about twenty of them and from their conduct they must all have been veteran pilots. After going a considerable distance past Huesca, they swung around in a wide turn and formed a long line over the enemy trenches. Little white smoke puffs indicated that the Fascists had finally got a few anti-aircraft guns up to that front, but the pilots of those bombers paid no attention whatever to them. By cutting their bombs loose in batches, instead of all at once, each of the Rasantes took care of about 200 yards of trench. By the use of those tactics they were able to demolish more than two miles of the enemy's trenches.

When the Rasantes finished their work we escorted them back into our territory and then went back and cruised around for a while looking for trouble—which didn't materialise. I suppose that the Fascists were still patching up the holes in planes and pilots, souvenirs of the fight of the day before. We managed to use up most of our surplus bullets, though, on the Fascists in the secondary trenches down below. Our planes traveled so fast that it was almost comical to see the efforts of the enemy gunners down below; they couldn't even come close to any of our planes. After playing around with them awhile we went back to the home field and called it a day.

The sixteenth of June, during which we made four flights, was our busiest day on that front. All four of these flights were with Rasantes and our only enemy opposition came on the third one. On that flight about fifty Heinkels and Fiats came down on top of us out of the sun, and then we dog-fought all over the sky for well over half an hour. At one point in this fight I saw a Fiat trying to dive down on our Rasantes, so I cut over to intercept him. He saw me coming in and banked around to meet me; but once more luck was with me in a head-on affair. My bullets practically tore his motor to pieces and must have got the unfortunate Italian pilot too, because even after he swung his plane around in line with mine he didn't fire a single shot. I turned to finish the job, but he was already headed for the ground 8000 feet below, with the usual trail of black smoke marking his path. His plane finally burst into flames with a violent explosion, and as I did not see his chute blossom out, I assume that he went down with his ship. Those monoplanes of ours certainly could spray the bullets out. That, incidentally, was my fifth enemy plane.

Within ten minutes the fight was over and we were in control of the air. During these ten minutes, though, I managed to get in bursts at several other enemy planes on their way down to the safety of their own territory. They were all in such terrifically fast dives, however, that it was next to impossible to do any accurate shooting. The final result of this fight wasn't as good as that of two days before. They only lost five of their planes, while we lost one of our Rasantes. The Rasante's motor had been put out of commission by explosive bullets, and when the pilot made his forced landing he forgot to cut his switch, and the plane caught fire in the ensuing crash. We saw the thing burning as we were going home. One of the monoplanes in my squadron was also riddled with bullets but the pilot wasn't hurt. The plane's mechanic, with Smoothie's assistance, had it ready for service again within an hour.

Two days later we did our last actual offensive work on that front. We made only one flight, but on that one flight we used practically everything we had available. There were three squadrons of Rasantes and two squadrons of Katiuskas, about fifty bombers in all. Then there were two squadrons of biplane fighters and three squadrons of monoplane fighters, about sixty fighting-planes. In other words, we had an aggregate of something over a hundred planes of all types.

On this occasion, we bombed Huesca proper for the first and only time. That one bombardment, however, was enough to last it for quite a while; it was the most thorough I have ever seen. Practically every part of the city had bombs dropped on it. When the bombers left, all that could be seen of Huesca was a huge cloud of black smoke rising from the wreckage of the city.

After the bombers finished their work, the fighters began strafing the trenches around the city, especially those in the rather large cemetery. Ukov and I were coming up after one of these strafing dives when a burst of anti-aircraft fire exploded about forty feet behind my plane. It was nothing but a matter of luck that I wasn't struck by any of the fragments. Ukov, however, had seen the flashes of the guns, which were located in a church belfry. We were so close to them that it would have been rather dangerous to try dodging them as usual, so we banked around and went for them, with our guns hammering away for all they were worth. This maneuver was a stroke of genius; the surprised gunners were in a hail of bullets before they even realized what was happening; they didn't have a chance. As soon as we flashed past the belfry we clutched for the ground and then went far enough back into our own territory to be out of range of other guns before climbing for altitude. Our escape was facilitated by the dense clouds of smoke that were drifting over into our territory. My last glimpse of Huesca showed it as a shattered and burning city, almost completely hidden by a pall of brownish-black smoke. When we got back to the field we were told to get ready to leave for Los Alcázares the following day.

The morning of the nineteenth found us all set to leave—but it was not to be. Shortly after we arrived at the field we saw one of the most horrible sights (for us) of the entire war. Lichnikov— "Old Sourpuss" as Baumler and I called him—had been having trouble with his plane and decided to go up and give it a test hop before leaving for Los Alcázares. He started out with fairly easy maneuvers and gradually worked up into his test stunts. Finally, he came down in a roaring, screaming dive and started to pull out into a zoom. But just at the bottom of his zoom, almost directly over the field, about three feet of his left wing-tip folded over and tore off. The plane immediately went into a violent left spiral and headed for the ground. He was going so fast that the centrifugal force kept him pinned to the cockpit seat and he and his plane crashed head on into the ground right in the middle of the field, with all pilots of both squadrons looking on in horrified silence.

For about ten seconds everyone on the field was rooted to the ground; then we all rushed out on the field. Why we did it I don't know; we were all perfectly aware of the fact that the pilot was past all help; he had been making at least 350 miles an hour when he struck the ground. I arrived at the scene just as the ambulance crew was lifting the body on a stretcher. I don't think I had ever seen a human body so completely smashed up. Practically every bone was pulverized. When they put the body on a stretcher, one man was holding up an arm, and when he released it, it collapsed just like a deflated inner tube. Lichnikov had been slated to leave for his home in Russia as soon as we got to Los Alcázares. He had been serving on all fronts in Spain for more than eight months—longer than any other pilot in the squadron—but such is war.

After seeing that there was nothing we could do, we all went back to our planes to wait for the starting signal; but instead of that we saw our double-rocket emergency signal go soaring into the air from the field house. Getting into formation, we flew over to the little town of Sariñena, where they had had some sort of bombardment scare. We flew around the town for a while but saw nothing, so we went back home. By that time the authorities had decided that it would be best to wait until the next day to start out on our trip to Los Alcázares. My squadron had the remainder of the day off, so I spent the afternoon loafing and writing on the third balcony of our house in Barbastro.

The view from that balcony was one of the most beautiful I saw in Spain. It presented so peaceful a scene that a stranger would never have suspected that a major city was in the last stages of a modern siege only about eighteen miles away. Off to the north were the Pyrenees, behind which was France. Their immense bulk gave the atmosphere in between a hazy blue aspect, so that a nearer and smaller mountain range showed up only as a vague outline.

In the foreground were cultivated fields, the principal crop being wheat. Although it was still comparatively early in the year, the first crop had already been cut and the farmers, with their inevitable donkey carts, were moving about the fields gathering in the sheaves. The only thing that kept us from feeling completely satisfied was that we couldn't converse with the two extremely good-looking *señoritas* who were keeping our glasses filled. They were typical Catalonian brunettes, with dark hair, dark eyes and smooth, dark features. They could understand our Castilian, but they were accustomed to speaking the local dialect and had an Aragonian accent, so we couldn't understand them. Even at that, it was an ideal ending for a successful campaign.

The following day we managed to get off for Los Alcázares. This trip took in almost the entire length of Spain, so we were again forced to refuel. The ceiling was very low that day, which made the trip more interesting; we had to fly so low that we could see all the details of the various ships and coastal towns. We arrived at Los Alcázares field in the hottest part of the afternoon and managed to get ourselves thoroughly dusty taxiing around the field.

That was our last flight for the month of June but, considering that we had taken part in two campaigns since the first, we were entitled to a rest.

CHAPTER XIV

VACATION—AND TROUBLE

During the last week in June we had a few days off for a rest period. Baumler managed to get permission to go to Valencia, but I missed out on that deal. Goofy, three other Russians and I piled ourselves and our luggage into two cars and motored up the coast to Alicante. There we were told to go to special quarters four or five miles north, in the little village of San Juan de Alicante. We were quartered in what had been the country villa of a rich Alicante businessman who had been found to have Fascistic tendencies. It consisted of a beautiful three-story house surrounded by remarkably well-kept grounds, the whole being enclosed by a high stone wall. It was very appropriately called the Villa Rusia.

A young doctor, ably assisted by his wife, was in charge of the place. This young doctor, Diego, and his wife Carmen, were the most perfect hosts it has ever been my pleasure to meet. They immediately proceeded to make us feel at home and started planning things for us to do. The place was staffed by a gardener and his wife, two chauffeurs, and about six comely *señoritas*. Carmen's principal duty was the supervision of these *señoritas*, who worked around the house, making up the rooms, serving meals, and otherwise attending to the comfort of the guests. It seemed that the Government had reserved the Villa Rusia for the express purpose of providing a haven for foreign pilots when they were on rest periods.

Our usual schedule was to get up at 8:30 or 9, eat breakfast, and then go for a swim down at the beach. After that would come a fresh-water shower and a general loafing period until lunch time, which was usually about 2 o'clock in the afternoon. Then, if we cared to, we could go to Alicante or wander around the local village.

The usual thing, though, was a two- or three-hour *siesta*. After that we would read, write, play croquet, or play tennis on the excellent concrete tennis court. Then we would get cleaned up and sit around the parlor listening to the radio or playing parlor games. The evening meal would usually take on the appearance of a banquet, with all kinds of food, wines, liqueurs and brandies. After that would come another game or music session in the parlor. However, those so minded could take advantage of the moonlight shining through the arbor coverings of various garden seats placed around the spacious grounds, provided they were persuasive enough to talk one of the *señoritas* into the idea.

All this was too good to last; I finally came to grief on the twenty-fifth of June. The doctor, his wife and all the Russians went in to Alicante to go swimming and take in a show. This left me to my own devices out at the villa. I wrote a couple of letters and then, having nothing better to do, started an investigation of the wine and liquor pantry; sampling various strange concoctions which I had never seen before. I finally found a little stone jug of something—*Ginebra*, I believe—with mixture directions written upon it in French. One sip convinced me that it had to be mixed with something, so I went to work. However, I think I must have got my directions mixed, because within five minutes after downing the resulting masterpiece I was afire inside. I immediately dashed out into the village and poured several glassed of cold vermouth on top of the conflagration. That treatment succeeded admirably, as I felt much better afterward.

All would have been well but for the fact that there was a bicycle shop next to the bar-room I had been using as a fire station. As soon as I saw it, I decided that I needed a bicycle in my business. The result of that decision was the purchase of an ancient relic which had the appearance of being at least fifteen years old. The dealer, however, assured me that there was no better *bicicleta* in the entire province. After pedaling around the village for a while I conceived the brilliant idea of breezing up the coast to Valencia, which I believed to be only about 30 miles away. (NB, I later discovered that it was all of 155). So away I went, pedaling at what I believed to be a furious rate of speed. I had to get off and push the bicycle up some of the hills, but I made excellent time on the down grades. Anyway, by midnight I was all of fifteen miles up the coast and still going strong.

All would still have been well if the bicycle had had the orthodox type of American brakes, but the thing had the usual European type operated by a lever on the handlebars. I went charging down one very steep hillside and found a little town at the bottom of it. The usual two guards stepped out into the middle of the road and one of them shouted, "*¡Alto!*" I forgot all about my handlebar brakes and started back-pedaling, with no results at all—except that I ran over one of the guards and the other one shot me down off my bicycle. Fortunately he had a small-caliber pistol and the bullet caught me far enough to the right of my mid-section to miss all vital parts. I remember thinking how ironic it was that I should be able to go through campaigns on five major fronts without getting a scratch and then get myself shot down off a bicycle, far back of the lines, by a civilian guard.

When they discovered that I was a pilot in one of the almost deified Russian fighter squadrons they were almost pitifully apologetic and woe-begone. I was taken immediately to the local first-aid station and temporarily patched up. Then, the only car in town—the mayor's—was commandeered for the purpose of hauling me to the military hospital in Alicante.

Before I ever entered Spain I had heard that the Spanish doctors ranked with the best in Europe, and the efficient way in which I was handled convinced me that the rumor was correct. As soon as I entered the hospital at Alicante I was given an anti-tetanus shot in one arm and a shot of something else in the other. Then the wound was thoroughly sterilized and bandaged. After that I was given a cup of hot, sweet goat's milk and put to bed for the night.

The next day I was given a more thorough examination. The head doctor came around and prodded around for a while with various fiendish instruments. He finally ascertained that the bullet had passed completely through my right side, just below the ribs, and had barely grazed the edge of the abdominal cavity. That eased my mind considerably, as I had been having all kinds of wild visions concerning a major operation.

That afternoon Baumler, who had just returned from Valencia, came over to the hospital to visit me. With him was another visitor who really surprised me—no other than Whitey Dahl, whom I had last seen at Azuqueca on the twenty-third of March. Dr. Diego also came along with them, and he seemed greatly perturbed over the amount of trouble I had managed to get myself into while technically under his care.

Whitey had been having quite a bit of trouble since I had last seen him. When he arrived at Valencia from the front in March he had persuaded the Air Ministry to give him permission to go to Paris. He had consulted the doctors at the American Hospital there about his stomach ailment, and they had informed him that he was suffering from appendicitis. So he went to the operation table. This would have been all right, but his letters of explanation to the Air Ministry had never been delivered and they thought he had merely decided not to come back. This had especially displeased LaCalle, who believed that he had been taken advantage of. Somehow or other, however, Whitey had managed to persuade them into allowing him to return to duty, and there he was.

The head doctor of the hospital finally came along and shooed my visitors out of the ward. They left some English novels and some American cigarettes, both of which were greatly appreciated. I managed to finish one of the books before the end of the day.

That evening I made the acquaintance of a few of my ward mates. I almost fell out of bed when I discovered that the occupant of a bed right across from mine was an American—a real American. He was an Indian from Oklahoma with the name of Morrison. And a couple of beds away from him was an English-speaking Negro from Jamaica. That made at least three English-speaking people in the ward, so the future began to look a little brighter. The other twenty-three patients in the ward turned out to be Spaniards. We had an exceptionally good-looking nurse who was one of the few natural blondes I saw in Spain. She certainly knew her business. She weighed only about 120 pounds, but I saw her pick up a patient one day who weighed at least 175 and carry him about forty feet to his bed.

The next morning I lured Morrison, the Indian, over to my bed, using the American cigarettes for bait, and we had a long talk. It was during this talk that I found out, to my amazement, that he was the American-speaking officer who had saved Finnick's life on the Segovia front. He had been in charge of the outfit from which the squad that found Finnick had come. On that particular day he had heard a sudden outbreak of Spanish oaths, intermingled with good old American cuss-words and, when he arrived on the scene, had found Finnick just on the verge of being shot as a German pilot. He had called off his men barely in time and had had Finnick carried to the emergency hospital. Then he had seen to it that word was sent to the headquarters of the squadron with which he was connected.

Morrison's own personal story was even more interesting. He had shipped aboard a merchant vessel at New Orleans and had arrived at Valencia only two days before the revolution broke out. He had been on shore leave when the shooting started and was left behind when his ship left hastily at the outbreak of hostilities. So he went out on the seacoast and lived on shellfish for three days, before hunger drove him back into Valencia for a change of diet. There he was taken in by a kind-hearted Loyalist and given a good meal. After the meal his host gave him a rifle and the pair of them went out to do battle against the Fascists in the streets of Valencia.

Morrison received two head wounds at Valencia, but after a short period of hospitalization he was able to join in the general march to the aid of Madrid. He arrived in Madrid in time to take part in the heroic defense which saved the city, but was seriously wounded and was sent back to Valencia to convalesce. By that time, on account of the extraordinary valor he had demonstrated, he had been advanced to the rank of second Lieutenant.

He stayed in the hospital at Valencia until his condition reached the stage considered by Indians as constituting complete recovery. That is, with the aid of a pair of crutches he was able to get to the nearest highway, where he was further able to hitch-hike to Madrid and finally return to his old outfit. He arrived just as they were being sent to the Segovia front, so he went along with them. In fact, when he appeared to save Finnick's life he was still wearing a pair of home-made braces.

Shortly after the Finnick incident he led his men against an enemy machine-gun emplacement and was laid up again. While their attention was directed against the original gun, another one surprised them with a raking crossfire. Morrison shouted to his men to take cover but he was a little too late himself. He managed to find a depression in the ground and lay down in it, but it was so shallow that his entire right side was showing above all protection. Then the cross-firing machine gun proceeded to do the best job of perforating a human being that I have ever seen. A series of bullet holes started at Morrison's right shoulder and worked on down to his right foot, there being at least ten of them.

When I saw him in the hospital he had already got over most of the body wounds, but a couple of the leg wounds had landed over older wounds and were causing quite a bit of trouble. He showed me a little envelope containing bone fragments, all of which had been taken from his right leg. The doctor took two or three of them out while I was there. Morrison told several of his more interesting experiences, intimating that the least the Government could do would be to allow Indian volunteers to take a few scalps every now and then. "It's a helluva war," he added, "when a fellow has to collect parts of his own bones to prove that he's been in it."

One of the experiences he related was this. He and his men were on duty on one of the fronts, with a little creek separating them from the Fascist militiamen. Every morning, at a certain time, the Fascists sent a four-man detail down to the creek for water. They thought they were using a secret route, but Morrison's Indian cunning soon enabled him to find out more about their route than they knew themselves. One morning he and three of his men armed themselves with two pistols apiece and went down and ambushed this water detail. They waited until one of the four Fascists was opposite each one of them and then they cut loose, instantly killing all four. Morrison's chief gripe seemed to be that all the money they found on the four corpses was either blood-stained or of Franco's worthless issue.

The head doctor had placed me on a liquid diet—which consisted of a large cup of hot, sweet goat's milk every two hours—day and night. He had also taken the precaution of leaving definite instructions with the nurse, so that I was never able to convince her that wine was a liquid diet. However, Morrison would ease out to the kitchen every now and then and filch a couple of glassfuls. I shall never forget the painful scene which occurred when the nurse caught us at it. I immediately took cover by claiming that I couldn't understand a word she was saying, thereby leaving Morrison to bear the brunt of the attack. He, in turn, managed to wriggle out by claiming that he hadn't known that I wasn't supposed to have any wine. This was such a good alibi that I forgot I wasn't supposed to understand what they were talking about and promptly backed up Morrison's statement. The nurse was so enraged at this revelation of my duplicity that she reported the pair of us to the head doctor. This, in turn, enraged us to the point where we insulted both the nurse and the doctor and informed them that we were ready to leave their blankety-blank hospital at any time if they didn't like our actions. Finally, Baumler, Whitey and Dr. Diego came in from the Villa Rusia and succeeded in negotiating a temporary halt in the hostilities.

Another incident in the Chang episode occurred while I was there in the hospital. It seemed that Chang had an aunt living near Alicante and had spent a bit of time in that vicinity. Anyway, during visitors' hour one day, two rather good-looking girls came in and asked to see the American aviator. It turned out that one of them had been Chang's pre-war sweetheart and thought that I might have known him, as he had mentioned in a letter from the front that he was flying with an American patrol. She was almost overcome with joy when I informed her that I had known him very well and showed her a few group pictures by way of proving it. But when she asked if I knew anything concerning his whereabouts I didn't have the heart to tell her the truth. I skirted it closely, though, by telling her that I wasn't sure where he was, but thought he might be in Valencia. I eased my conscience by giving her a couple of pictures of Chang, one showing him alone by his plane and the other showing him with Whitey and me. As she had no other pictures of him, she left feeling completely happy.

Every afternoon Baumler, Whitey, and most of the other boys

came to the hospital for a visit, bringing books, cigarettes and anything else they happened to think of. Baumler and Whitey also spent a lot of time talking to Morrison and became quite interested in his story. Every time that Dr. Diego came with them I asked him to try to get me transferred out to the Villa Rusia, and he finally managed to swing the deal.

On the twenty-ninth of June, after four days in the hospital, I was transferred out to the Villa. That night I had my first square meal. The remarkable thing was that I had gained over five pounds in the four days of that liquid diet of goat's milk and wine. We had an excellent meal that night, which would have been perfect if Goofy hadn't insisted on having me sit on his right, where he could personally supervise my wine consumption. It was a sort of farewell banquet, as all the rest of the boys were to leave for Los Alcázares the next day. From there the squadron was to return to duty on the Madrid front.

The next morning Baumler, Whitey and the Russians piled into cars and returned to Los Alcázares, while I was left at the Villa Rusia to recuperate. I was the only guest left in the place after they left. But since I had Dr. Diego, his wife Carmen, the six *señoritas* and the kitchen staff to look after me, I suppose that it could have been worse.

My pistol and bicycle were still in possession of the local authorities of the little town where I had been shot. On July first I borrowed the doctor's V-8 and went up there to see about getting them back. When we arrived we had to wait about two hours until the mayor returned from Alicante before my belongings could be obtained. Upon our return to the Villa Rusia, Dr. Diego informed me that at least another week would be necessary for my complete recovery.

That night I met a young Spaniard who could speak English! He was Manuel Giner de los Ríos, nephew of the Spanish ambassador to the United States. He was in charge of one of the colonies of children who had been evacuated from Madrid. He told me that he expected to be sent to the United States with a shipload of children at some time in the near future. We had a very interesting talk after the evening meal, in both Spanish and English. He was a little rusty at English conversation, so at times we found it more convenient to shift over to Spanish. It was after midnight before he took his departure.

My recuperation was cut short the next morning when Goofy called up from Los Alcázares and said I was to report there for duty at once. I immediately packed up my few personal belongings, gave my bicycle to Manuel's colony of children and set off for Los Alcázares in the doctor's car. In spite of the fact that we had a flat tire and ran over a donkey cart, we managed to arrive about the middle of the afternoon. I located Baumler and Whitey at the officers' quarters bar and found that they were having troubles of their own; Whitey was having trouble, anyway. He had expected that he would be put into monoplanes with Baumler and me, but the high command deemed that he go back to duty in the biplanes for a while.

Our orders finally came through on the Fourth of July, but we Americans refused to go to the field that day, claiming that since it was our national holiday we felt in duty bound to observe it in a fitting manner. We therefore gathered together three Very pistols, with a supply of colored flares. We would vary this procedure at times, though, by firing off a salvo with our service pistols and singing as much of *The Star Spangled Banner* as we could remember. All that we lacked was an American flag to hoist. The natives, of course, thought we were hopelessly insane, but they had been of that opinion for a long time, anyway. Our conduct that day merely strengthened their convictions.

Baumler and I finally took off the next day with two squadrons of monoplanes for the Guadalajara Valley. Many of the old Russian pilots had been replaced by new ones who weren't nearly as good at the controls. Two of them cracked up when we landed at an intermediate field to refuel. One of them merely tore up his landing gear, but the other completely wrecked his plane. He overshot the field and crashed into a bank across the road that ran along on side of it. He was dying as we took off on the second leg of the trip. When we arrived over the Guadalajara Valley, the other squadron landed at Alcalá de Henares, while we went over to the old commercial field at Barajas, which is about twelve miles north-east of Madrid. Before the war it had been the principal airport for Madrid.

Later that day all pilots were loaded into cars and taken over to inspect a field we were to use later. It was away up on the side of the Sierra Guadarrama and turned out to be the same field I had inspected before, near the little town of Manzanares de la Sierra. It had looked small for biplanes and looked even smaller for monoplanes.

That night my bullet wound was worse, probably from the side-strain of hoisting myself and my parachute in and out of the plane. Anyway, the squadron doctor had me turn in at the Barajas clinic the next morning. The remainder of the squadron went on over to the field we had inspected the evening before. When they were landing, another one of the new pilots turned his plane over. Then, that afternoon, still another came in to Barajas and dropped about fifteen feet, completely wrecking his plane. Neither pilot was seriously injured. I believe the reason for these many crack-ups by new pilots was that they had been trained on sea-level fields. Anyway, they didn't seem to be able to realize that higher landing speeds were necessary when landing on high-altitude fields on account of the decreased density of the atmosphere. The field up in the Sierra was at least 4000 feet above sea level, which made quite a difference in the landing speed of the monoplanes.

The following morning another of the new pilots squashed in on the field and cracked up. He was very severely injured; the doctor thought he might have suffered a concussion of the brain. A little later another pilot was hauled in with a couple of anti-aircraft fragments through the seat of his pants. An anti-aircraft shell had exploded directly beneath his plane, which was lucky for him, as the two fragments had to pass through his parachute before getting to him. His wounds, though very painful, were not serious.

At noon the doctor decided that I was in good enough condition to ride over to Manzanares in an automobile. The hole in my back was completely cured, but the one in front was still a little infected. I arrived at the field just in time for the noon meal, and then went in to the little village and spent the remainder of the day at the pilots' house.

I was pleased to discover that my two old friends from Campo

X, María and Cristina, were among the girls assigned to the caretaking of the house. It had been over two months since I had seen them. They had heard rumours of my getting shot, and naturally inferred that it had been in an airplane. We sat around for the rest of the afternoon drinking Málaga wine and talking over old times.

The house there at Manzanares was a fairly new one. It was a rather small, square, two-story affair, but there was plenty of room in it for our small number of squadron members. Baumler and I lived in a room at the head of the stairs, a very handy situation. The best thing about the place was that it was very cool at night, a great relief after the stifling nights at Barajas and Los Alcázares.

One patrol took off, July eight, on a reconnaissance flight over the territory directly in front of Madrid. They were pretty well shot up by anti-aircraft and one of them, Beliekov, was wounded rather badly in the right shoulder. When he took off his flying jacket there was a large jagged sliver of steel sticking out of that shoulder. The hospital corpsman got out his surgical tweezers and began tugging at the sliver, much to the discomfort of Beliekov. Goofy saw that the corpsman wasn't getting anywhere, so he equipped himself with a large pair of mechanic's pliers and with one mighty heave did the job. Beliekov was then bandaged up and sent in to the hospital in Madrid.

Late that afternoon we took off and escorted about fifteen Rasantes over past Madrid. They did a fair job of bombarding the trenches near Villa de Cañada. When they were safely on their way home we went back and machine-gunned the enemy trenches at Casa de Campo—directly in front of Madrid. Shortly after we landed we heard that our troops were doing excellent work up at the front. They had completely surrounded a large body of Moroccans and had captured a lot of equipment. I have always wondered what happened to captive Moroccans over there. They were certainly the objects of unbelievable hatred on the part of civilian non-combatants in our territory.

Later on in the day Whitey came over from Alcalá to see Baumler and me. He had Alberto, an English-Spanish interpreter from the Air Ministry, along with him. The interpreter had been at Alcalá a couple of days and still didn't know exactly what they were going to do with him. We cheered him up with assurances that he would soon be with us and changed the subject to our own troubles. Baumler had been having some kind of glandular trouble in his throat, which had been gradually swelling until he could no longer fasten his flying-jacket collar. It was also giving him trouble whenever we had to fly at high altitudes. All I had to gripe about was the pain in my right side, but it was gradually decreasing.

Whitey and Alberto stayed over for supper and we had wild duck on the menu. The Madrid reservoir lake was right by the side of our field and there were always two or three flocks of wild ducks on it. Goofy had taken a shotgun and gone out and killed several of them that afternoon. Later on we started machine-gunning them whenever we came back from a mission with any bullets left over. After we had made a few passes at them the mechanics would paddle out and pick up the victims. These made a very welcome addition to our usual diet. The ducks resembled, and tasted like, our own American mallards. It was out of season at the time, but we didn't think there was much danger of running into a game warden there.

We saw a very unusual sight that night when the Junkers came over and bombed Alcalá and Barajas. We were so far up the mountainside that it was just as though we were watching a grandiose theatrical production. When our searchlights went into action and began playing across the sky, the rear gunners of the Junkers opened fire on them. Their tracer bullets made beautiful patterns which, in conjunction with the searchlights and the anti-aircraft bursts, made an unforgettable night. The show lasted for over two hours and was enjoyed by everyone—with the possible exception of the citizens of Alcalá and Barajas.

The citizens of Alcalá however had perfected a pretty good scheme for protecting themselves in the rather frequent bombing raids. They had dug regular cave apartments in the sides of the hills across the Henares river from the city, and it was their custom to spend their nights in the safety of these caves and then return to their regular businesses the next morning. In fact, I noticed these cliff dwellings all over Loyalist territory outside of the larger towns and cities. So there is a possibility that the next world conflict may drive us back to the cliff-dwelling stage. It's something to think about, anyway. Some of these caves which I examined outside of Alcalá were just as spacious and comfortable as some of the houses. They must have been very comfortable in the heat of the day.

The following day we made two flights over the lines; both of them being made with squadrons of Rasantes. On the first flight we escorted about twelve of them over to Navalcarnero, about thirteen miles southwest of Madrid. After they dropped their bombs we went down and machine-gunned the city. There was so much anti-aircraft fire, though, that we scrammed after our first pass and went over to the poor Fascists in the trenches at Casa de Campo and strafed them until we were almost out of bullets. Goofy ground-looped beautifully when we landed, thus putting another plane out of commission. That afternoon we took about fifteen Rasantes over and waited around until another squadron of about twelve came over and followed them up. Then we machine-gunned the boys at Casa de Campo again. After that we called it a day and went home—taking time out over the lake to kill a few ducks for supper.

On July tenth we again made two flights. Our first was the usual escorting of Rasantes, but the second was a double-rocket emergency alarm. Yet when we arrived at the front we could see nothing, so we amused ourselves by diving down on the enemy trenches near Brunete and strafing the Fascists. On one of these dives a burst of anti-aircraft went off about thirty feet to the left of my plane. It broke the left side of my wind-shield and riddled the left side of the plane, but fortunately neither the motor nor myself was injured. My Arkansas luck was still holding up. That was as close as enemy anti-aircraft ever got to my plane. That night we had the usual bombardment but it was completely ignored by all hands.

There were no flights the next day as all of the planes in our squadron were being given a routine overhaul. Baumler and I got a car and went over to Alcalá to see Whitey, but found that he had been assigned to a biplane squadron over at our old field at Campo Soto. We arrived at Soto in time for the evening meal, but were too late to meet Whitey, who had just left for Madrid to look for us. We dashed in to Madrid and finally met Whitey in the lobby of the Hotel Florida. He was feeling very disconsolate; all the other pilots in his squadron were new Russian replacements who couldn't even speak Spanish, so he had no one to talk to.

We also met two officers from the Lincoln Brigade, Lieutenant Land and Captain Dart, and the five us decided to make a night of it. We went around to a bootlegging establishment and bought five bottles of champagne and then went to the dining salon of the Hotel Gran Vía. We had a second snack there, accompanied by table wine, and then settled down to our champagne, which had been cooling off in a bucket of ice under the table. All would have been well except for the fact that there were five Spanish militia officers at the next table, with five very good-looking *señoritas*, and we decided to try to get the ladies over to our table. The fight started when we finally succeeded. We had a regular old-fashioned free-for-all for about five minutes, and then one of the militia officers tried to pull out his pistol. All five of us immediately pulled out our guns and started firing into the ceiling; whereupon all five of our erstwhile opponents vanished. Unfortunately, all five of the ladies also vanished, leaving us to nurse our various bruises and black eyes. That was the end of the party. Baumler and I dropped Whitey off at Campo Soto and then went on to our own house at Manzanares. That was the last time we saw Whitey.

We had a rather embarrassing time the next morning when we showed up with our bruises and black eyes. Goofy intimated that we were setting a deplorable example for the younger pilots. The fracas hadn't helped Baumler's throat any; it was much worse than before. Fortunately, our planes were still under repair, so we didn't have to fly until late in the afternoon. Two of the squadrons at Alcalá went out in the morning, however, and got into the first dogfight of that campaign. Three of our planes were shot down but they managed to get eight Fiats and one Heinkel, so they could have done worse. They reported that they had seen a new German monoplane fighter in action for the first time, which gave us something to think about.

CHAPTER XV

MY LAST DOGFIGHTS

We saw our first enemy fighting-planes on that front on July thirteenth and made three flights with quite a bit of action on each. On our first flight we went out with a squadron of Katiuskas, and just after they finished their bombardment we ran into five Italian bi-motored bombers—Romeos. Their pilots were evidently rather timid: they were flying 5000 feet higher than our Katiuskas had been. We chased them ten or twelve miles but never could get within effective machine-gun range.

Our second flight was with two squadrons of Rasantes and a squadron of Katiuskas. It was marked by the most intensive anti-aircraft fire we had seen up to that time; yet they were unable to bring down a single one of our planes, which must have been rather discouraging. As no enemy planes made their appearance, we went over to Casa de Campo and took it out on them. In fact, one of our general rules was to machine-gun the enemy trenches whenever we were fired on by anti-aircraft guns. We figured that the trench troops would put two and two together and get tired of that performance.

Our third flight that day was by far the best. We went over with our bombers and were attacked by practically the entire enemy air force. The ensuing dogfight lasted for well over an hour; and we got our first glimpse of the new enemy monoplanes. At one point in this flight I saw one of our biplanes, all by itself, being attacked by three of these new monoplanes. I had a couple of new Russian pilots flying on my wings, so I led them over to the rescue. Before we could get there, however, the biplane started smoking furiously and going down, evidently out of control. I managed to get on the tail of the leading enemy monoplane and pumped bullets into it until it burst into flames. While I was doing this my two wing men, whom I had shifted over into right echelon, got on the tail of the right monoplane and sent it down out of control—a nice piece of teamwork for green pilots. The plane on the left, though, managed to make good its escape.

When we returned to the field I reported that one of our biplanes had been shot down and that the pilot had gone down with his plane. You can imagine how I felt when I was informed that the unfortunate pilot was Whitey Dahl. The only consolation I had was that we had got two of the three planes which had attacked him. Our losses in that fight had been one biplane and two monoplanes; but we had shot down an assortment of twelve Fiats, Heinkels and new German monoplanes we called *Mayser-Schmidts* (these were Messerschmitt Bf 109B's). Needless to say, Baumler and I weren't feeling any too good when we turned in that night. We blamed the high command for putting Whitey off in a squadron where he couldn't possibly understand any of the orders given.

July fourteenth, my birthday, was also very interesting—a three-flight day. Our first two flights were the usual ones with bombers, but when we came in from the second one we found that there was too strong a cross-wind to land in. I went over to Alcalá and landed—and discovered that the rest of the squadron had gone to Barajas. After trying vainly to rejoin my squadron, I ended by going to Madrid and sleeping in the Palace of Fine Arts.

The fifteenth was an extremely busy day. In the morning I took off and started again looking for my squadron. I went first to Alcalá, but as I didn't see any of our squadron numbers on the planes there, I headed south for Campo Real—and there they were! Goofy started to give me a good bawling out, but just as he was getting a full head of steam, five enemy bombers showed up over the field and we all had to take off. They missed the field with their bombs, but they were too high for us to have any chance of catching them. We landed and Goofy started on his bawling out again; but just about that time the anti-aircraft guns at Alcalá started popping away and there were five more bombers. They were evidently a new development of the German Junkers, as they were much faster than any of the other enemy bombers we had seen before. We managed, however, to get over to Alcalá in time to head off the raiders and drive them off. They dropped their bombs, but these landed so far wide of the mark that it was evident that they were merely unloading to make better speed.

Those bombers were brand new ones of the bi-motored type. They would cross the lines at a very high altitude and then throttle down their motors and go into a sort of half-power glide, sneaking up on their objective with as little noise as possible. By using these tactics they were usually able to get right over one of our fields before being detected. They would then do their bombing, push their noses down and head for home with both motors wide open. Fortunately, they had to do their bombing at such high altitudes that they were very inaccurate.

On our fourth flight of the day we escorted about eighteen of our Rasantes over the lines to Brunete. They laid down a line of bombs which cut across the northern edge of the town and set something afire which made an awful smoke. We escorted the Rasantes safely back across the lines and then went over to Casa de Campo for our usual bit of ground-strafing; but just as we were about to settle down to work we were attacked by a whole swarm of Fiats and Heinkels. The ensuing dogfight lasted about half an hour and was directly over Madrid most of the time. I fired at about a dozen planes but didn't have time to see if any of them hit the ground. The monoplane boys from Alcalá soon showed up and between us we had the sky cleared up in short order. We then resumed our work at Casa de Campo and used up the remainder of our bullets on the Fascist ground troops. When reports came in from Madrid we found that our combined squadrons had shot down eleven Heinkels and Fiats, while our losses had been two biplanes and one monoplane.

Baumler's throat had swollen up so much by this time that the doctor ordered him to Valencia for treatment. As he was to leave in the morning, we went over to Campo Soto for Whitey's personal effects that night. We also tried to decide the question of who was to write to Mrs Dahl, up in Paris, and tell her of her husband's death. We finally agreed that each of us would write a letter.

At one time during the day an amusing incident occurred. We were getting ready to take off to escort Rasantes and all of us were standing by our planes with parachutes. Goofy's plane was on one side of the control shack and my plane was on the other. All our planes had already been warmed up except Goofy's which was still running; so that he could hear nothing but his motor. He was also talking to Baumler, who had been ordered from duty by the doctor. The rest of us heard the familiar sound of motors roaring up in the air and, upon looking up, saw that it was caused by two of our own Katiuskas flying directly over the field. Baumler had also noticed them but had said nothing to Goofy about them. At just about that time our starting rocket was fired, and of course Goofy started a bit, as did all of us in those tense days. He asked Baumler, in a joking manner, what the cause of the rocket was and Baumler, also joking, said, "*Aparatos de bombardeo!*" (bombing planes) and pointed up at our two bi-motored bombers. Goofy took one startled look and, seeing that they were twin-motored planes and not the single-motored ones we were expecting, started for the bomb shelter so fast that his parachute was actually trailing out behind him. The shelter was about a hundred feet from his plane, but he made it in not more than two seconds and went down into it with an audible swish. When it was explained to him that the rocket had only been our own starting signal, a more sheepish-looking person would have been hard to find.

Baumler left for Valencia the next morning taking Whitey's gear along with him. He made the trip in a large Ford tri-motored transport. My squadron didn't fly that day, as our planes were being overhauled again. The extremely hot weather and the dusty fields caused them to need frequent overhaulings. My motor, especially, had more hours of flying time than was good for it and gave me a lot of trouble. That afternoon Goofy and two of the other old pilots were relieved by new Russian pilots. The new men hadn't learned to speak Spanish very well, so I had to talk to them through an interpreter.

Alcalá was bombed again that morning, but all the bombs fell clear of the field; however, José, the Russian commander of the aviation units in the Guadalajara valley, was standing outside the bomb shelter watching the show and was slightly wounded in the leg by a far-flying fragment. All the pilots of my squadron went over to Alcalá for the noon meal and then went in to Madrid for a bath. We then returned to Campo Real and, after supper, saw a fine bombardment before turning in for the night. There were bombers all over the sky, and we had many more searchlights, so they put up a fine show for a while. This was an excellent commendation for the work we had been doing against Franco's air service; they were trying their best to put our planes out of commission at night, and were merely wasting their more or less expensive Italian and German bombs. The little town of Campo Real was right on the edge of the plateau overhanging the Guadalajara valley, so we again had a ringside seat for the nightly bombardments.

In a half-hour dogfight with the new German monoplanes (*Mayser-Schmidts*) on the seventeenth I found out several things about them. They could out-dive our own monoplanes on account of their better streamlined water-cooled motors, but we were faster on the straightaway and could outclimb and outmaneuver them. I discovered most of this when I got behind one of them which was diving down on a patrol of our biplanes. When the pilot became aware of his imminent danger, he pulled up and tried a climbing turn—a fatal error. I tacked on to his tail and played my machine guns like an accordion. His motor finally burst into flames and he took to his parachute, so I turned my attention elsewhere. My two Russian wing men were still in position when we came out of that maneuver; which spoke well of their training in Russia. Our score for that fight wasn't so good—only five planes. We had shot down one of the Junkers bombers, two Heinkels and two of the new *Mayser-Schmidts*. Our only loss turned out to be one of our biplanes with a new Russian pilot.

There were a few Fiats up above, but they didn't come down and join in the festivities. We had noticed before that they were particularly bashful about closing in. Whenever we identified enemy planes as Fiats we merely pointed all our planes in their direction and opened fire. Mussolini's boys didn't seem to be able to stand up under fire. They would usually try to run, and the rest would be easy. The German pilots, though, were very evidently the best-trained pilots in Spain; but they did not have the equipment. They always tried to put up a fight with what they had, though. If the German pilots had had the equipment that the Italian pilots had, there would have been an entirely different story after each dogfight. If we pointed our planes at German planes they would point theirs right back, and then it would be a matter of luck and maneuverability as to who got whom. Our superior maneuverability was usually the deciding factor.

On July eighteenth we established a record and had our hardest day's work. We made three flights and had a dogfight on each one. On our first flight we took our Rasantes over the lines and were attacked by an assortment of Fiats and Heinkels. We immediately tore into the Fiats, sending them home on the run, and then went to work on the Heinkels. It took us a good half-hour to convince them that they had no business in that vicinity. I remember that in one of our wildest scrambles, with planes milling around all over the sky, there was a Heinkel pilot going down in his parachute. What must his thoughts have been? Absolutely unprotected and a mad whirl of planes whipping all around him. Anyway, we finally managed to clear the sky.

Our second flight was a rocket alarm. We dashed up to the front and found that two squadrons of the new German monoplanes had actually had the crust to come over and try strafing our own ground troops near Brunete. We caught them right down on the ground. We felt so badly about the matter that we shot five of them down before they made good their escape. We had always felt, up to that time, that if any trench-strafing was to be done, we were the ones to do it.

Our third flight was the best of all. We took nineteen of our bombers over and were attacked by everything that the enemy had in the air. The dogfight lasted for over an hour and covered a twenty-five mile stretch along the front lines, all the way from Madrid to El Escorial. At the very end of the flight I caught a Fiat skulking under the base of a large flat-bottomed cumulus cloud. Realizing that he couldn't hope to outclimb me, he did a half-roll and went into a vertical dive, but I had a little too much speed for him to be able to get away with it. I overshot a little in my half-roll but was able to pull back in line again, although I almost blacked out in the process. When I finished my firing he continued in his dive and crashed into the ground at a tremendous speed. I suppose the pilot was killed, because there was no smoke or vaporized gasoline trailing out behind his plane.

That plane, which brought my score up to eight, was the last that I shot down for the People's Air Corps. In fact, that was my last general dogfight in Spain. From that time on, the only planes I shot at were bombers. When reports came in from the front-line ground observers that night, we found that we had accounted for a total of eighteen enemy planes and had lost four of our own fighters in the three dogfights of the day. That was pretty close to the average so we went to bed feeling very well pleased.

A very peculiar thing occurred during the last dogfight that day. An enemy bi-motored bomber came buzzing through the thick of it just when it was at its worst. Its pilot had evidently been sent out on a reconnaissance before the fight started and didn't know what was going on until he was right in the middle of it. Practically every one of our planes took a pass at him before he could get clear. He was very fortunate in that we were too busy at the time to be able to pay much attention to him. Even at that, his plane must have been pretty well riddled.

The nineteenth was another busy day for us, with four flights. On our first flight with the usual Rasantes, one anti-aircraft shell made what was evidently a direct hit on one of our monoplanes. The monoplane was flashing along at about 250 miles an hour, and the shell must have exploded right in its gas tank, because it burned completely up in a space of about seventy-five yards. There was a fierce, brilliant-red flare for that distance, and then there was nothing to be seen except a sausage-shaped cloud of thick black smoke. The pilot had no chance at all, as the entire conflagration lasted only a second or two. That was the second plane that I had seen shot down by anti-aircraft and both of them had been got by direct hits, which proves that there is plenty of room for improvement in modern anti-aircraft guns. In spite of the increased volume of the enemy's fire, we still paid no attention to it. We could see the flash of their guns long before the shells arrived, and at the speed we were traveling it was child's play to dodge the shells.

Our second flight was a double-rocket alarm—enemy bombers

over Barajas. We arrived there too late; the criminals were already well on their way home before we even took off. Heavy clouds of powder smoke were drifting away from the field, exposing the burning skeleton of a Rasante which had been set afire by one of the bombs. It had cracked up on the field a few days before, so it wasn't any great loss.

Our third flight occurred when five Italian bombers showed up over Alcalá. We got there just in time to see the bombs working their way across the field; all the planes there had already taken off, though, so no damage was done. I was up at about 12,000 feet when I sighted an enemy bomber several thousand feet higher, headed in the opposite direction. I immediately pulled up on my propeller and started firing at it. This maneuver was a little too much for my over-worked motor and it stalled. I pushed over into a glide and went to work on the wobble pump, trying to start it again. There wasn't a sign of life, although the air speed of the glide I was in was keeping the motor turning over at about a thousand revolutions per minute. I finally lowered my wheels and got ready to make a forced landing at Alcalá, which was a little distance off to the right.

Just after coming to this decision I saw another line of bombs start working their way across the field and, upon looking up, saw that two more bombers were up above. I was just going into my field approach—at about 1500 feet—when the motor cut in again on about seven cylinders. So I immediately went home and started Gregoric and Pedro, my mechanic, to work on that motor.

They finished their emergency repairs just in time for me to get in on the last flight of the day—another enemy bombardment of Alcalá. Once more they were too high for us to catch up with. We flew around for a while, at high altitudes, until our gasoline began to run low, and then went home just before sunset. We had another bombardment that night but were too tired even to stay up and watch it.

Before sunrise on the twentieth, three different pairs of Junkers came over the field. I took off after the first pair, accompanied by my two new Russian wing men, and followed the German ships all the way to Guadalajara. We fired all our bullets at them but failed to bring either of them down. We were the cause, however, of an extremely unusual situation on the second one. At one time when we were firing at it, its right meter started smoking furiously, looking as if it were afire. The rear machine-gunner evidently thought it was afire, because he jumped out and tried to take to his parachute. He pulled his ripcord a little too soon, though, and the parachute hung up on the plane's tail assembly. The last time we saw them the plane was headed down in a long shallow dive towards its own territory with the luckless gunner still dangling helplessly from the tail surfaces.

We returned over Alcalá, on our way back to Campo Real, just in time to see the bombs of the second pair of planes cutting across one corner of the field. As we had no more bullets left, all we could do was sit up there and gawk. A line of bombs started falling east of the field, cut across the northeast corner, and the last ones fell almost due north of the field's center. The only damage done was to a Fiat fighter which had been brought over by a deserting Italian pilot a few days before. The third pair of planes had gone to work on the field at Barajas, but too late to do any damage; we had given the alarm in time for all of our planes to get off the ground before the bombers' arrival. One of the third pair of bombers was shot down, so they really came out on the losing end of the deal.

Late that afternoon we received word that five Junkers had been seen crossing the lines, headed in our direction, so off we went. We cruised around in the clouds for quite a while, and inasmuch as we didn't see them and they didn't bomb, we assumed that they had caught a glimpse of our planes and gone home. That night we went in to Madrid and slept at the Palace of Fine Arts; the big shots were evidently afraid that the enemy might know that we were at Campo Real.

The twenty-first of July, with five flights, was our busiest day of the war. Our first flight was wasted; two bombers came over our field and, when we got upstairs, we found that they were two of our own Katiuskas. We weren't taking any chances in those days. Our second flight occurred when two enemy observation planes passed over the field. They were both too high and too fast for us to get within firing range. We were to hear more from those two later on.

Our remaining three flights were the usual ones of escorting our own bombers across the lines. On each of these flights there was plenty of anti-aircraft fire, but we didn't see a sign of enemy fighting-planes. We figured that they had either run out of planes or were still busy patching up the holes received in the last dogfight. Each time, though, we used up our surplus bullets on the luckless Fascists in the trenches at Casa de Campo. On our third trip nothing but Providence saved us when we strafed the trenches. They were laying in wait for us and had every machine gun in that sector firing at us when we came down. Their tracer bullets made it look just like an inverted sleet storm. We whistled over to the comparative safety of the streets of Madrid and made our next two passes at altitudes high enough to keep clear of ordinary machine-gun bullets.

By this time all the old Russian pilots had been relieved by new ones who spoke very little Spanish, so I had no one at all to talk to except my Spanish mechanic and two Russian technical men, Gregoric and Smoothie. Even Goofy had been relieved by a new Russian pilot. So that night I decided to write to the Air Ministry and give them the required ten days' notice. I didn't mind the war, but the boredom of having no one to talk to was a little too much for me. I figured that with all the new pilots they were receiving they could very easily get along without my assistance. Six months at a stretch was all that the Russian pilots served, and I had already been there almost seven months.

That night I heard some very interesting news. The chief Russian interpreter in that vicinity made a special trip over to Campo Real and informed me that Whitey had landed unhurt in Fascist territory in his parachute and was a prisoner of Franco's at Salamanca. This was the best news I had heard in a long time. I still couldn't figure out how Whitey managed to get out of his plane safely. I suppose that while we were busy with the other three attacking planes he had taken to his chute and drifted so far away from the falling plane that we had failed to notice him. At any rate, I was able to tear up the various and sundry first drafts of letters of condolence to Mrs. Dahl. I thanked the stars that I had been too stupid to finish any of them.

The following day we were given another well-earned rest; our planes needed another dusting and overhauling. Having nothing better to do I got a car and went over to Alcalá to see if I had any mail. And, as usual, I managed to get myself into trouble. While I was at the field house at Alcalá we received a phone call informing us that two enemy bombers had been seen heading in our direction, so I filed down into the bomb shelter with the rest of the ground personnel and stayed there for about an hour. I then climbed out and started for Madrid. I had gone only about a hundred years before I heard our anti-aircraft guns open fire and heard the unmistakable whistle of heavy bombs coming down.

There was only one thing for me to do and that was to stop the car and dive for the gutter. Fortunately I was just about halfway between the two lines of bombs which the two enemy bombers were laying across that part of the field. I believe that that was my worst ten seconds in Spain.

I could hear the things whistling down and each one of them sounded as if it were right over me. And I couldn't do a thing except lie there and listen to the bloodcurdling whistles and the ear-splitting detonations. They were easy explosions to hear, too, inasmuch as the bombs were of the 225-pound type. Later I remembered that there had been a lot of débris falling around me, but at the time I didn't even notice it.

About ten minutes after the last explosion I climbed out of my gutter and scuttled off for Madrid as fast as my ancient flivver could scuttle. As I left the field I saw one of our monoplanes, which had been under repair, burning furiously. I supposed that the blast of a bomb had sent it afire. I was well on my way to Madrid when I noticed that my car's top was a wreck, completely riddled by bomb fragments, and that my erstwhile new pair of white trousers would never be the same again. I later found out that the bombardment had also destroyed a gasoline truck.

All this was forgotten, however, when I arrived at the Florida Hotel in Madrid. My old girl friend, Dolores, was still in town, so I called her up and we made the rounds of the night clubs. After that I went over to the Palace of Fine Arts, where the rest of the pilots were, and turned in for the night.

We arose long before daylight the next morning and went out

to Campo Real—and there the Italian bombers caught us by surprise. I noticed a lot of people running for the shelters and when I looked up there were two Romeos almost directly overhead. I hurriedly slipped on my parachute and jumped into the plane, which fortunately had an electric starter that worked. I was favored by fate again when the motor caught on the first turnover. I was already taking off when the two red flares went soaring up over the field house. As I cleared the ground I glanced back, just in time to see three bombs box the spot where my plane had been. Only two other pilots besides myself got off the ground; the rest of them got the alarm too late and most of them very wisely went to the bomb shelters. As we came around in our first turn, though, I saw a bomb burst directly in front of one of our planes which was taking off. The plane immediately nosed over and started sliding on its back.

The bombers were nearly 15,000 in the air, so we didn't stand a change of catching up with them. I fired at one of them, at a long distance, until both of my guns jammed, and then returned to the field. The new bomb craters, however, would have made landing very hazardous, so I led my two wing men over to Alcalá and landed. There we found out how much damage had been inflicted on our squadron by the bombardment.

The pilot of the plane which we had seen skidding along on its back had a miraculous escape. His motor had been entirely torn off, but he had got away with only one wound where a bomb fragment had sliced across his right shoulder. But we had lost Gregoric, our motor technician. A bomb had landed only about fifteen feet in front of him and had torn a huge hole in his left side. When he discovered the extent of the damage by fumbling around with his right hand, he pulled out a pistol and shot himself. Such was the spirit of the people I was fighting with. Two Spanish mechanics had been slightly wounded by fragments but everyone else had got away with nothing more than a bad fright.

We had supper at Barajas and then went to the Palace of Fine Arts to spend the night. The Government had really fixed up some fine quarters for us in that huge, thick-walled building, including rooms in the basement for the use of any pilots who happened to be on duty on the more exposed fields. There was even a swimming pool in the basement for anyone who cared to use it. The only disadvantage was that they had also stored the more valuable paintings and statues down there in our quarters. I always used the same room and at the foot of my bed, one on each side, stood life-sized statues of Venus and Adonis. It was quite an experience to wake up in the morning and be greeted by the sight of those two objects of art.

When I returned to the field at Barajas, the chief inspector came around, gave my plane its regular monthly inspection, and promptly condemned it. He informed me that, as far as he could figure out, the thing had been flying on nothing but its reputation for at least two weeks. According to him, the motor was shot, three or four of its base bolts were broken, the wheel retracting gear wasn't reliable and the machine guns were worn out. In addition, he stated with appropriate gestures that the fuselage was so full of anti-aircraft and bullet holes that it was as flexible as the accordion I was playing under the wing at the time.

He wanted to know why I hadn't reported the plane's condition, even going so far as to intimate that I had menaced his professional reputation by not doing so. As I could think of nothing better to say, I merely informed him that I liked my planes that way—and he stomped off, tearing his hear and muttering something about *americanos locos*. I had heard that phrase many times before, so I refused to be insulted. The inspector's temper wasn't at all soothed when I accompanied his stomping off with a few of the more military passages from *Rigoletto*. I suppose that if he had known it was Italian music we would have had a duel right then and there. Anyway, he went in and had a talk with the squadron's chief mechanic and their final decision was that I should fly the plane down to Los Alcázares and trade it in for a new model.

So the following morning I took off for Albacete with a very bad set of navigating maps. I arrived safely, though, just in time to have breakfast at the ex-Duke of Albacete's country home. After that I bummed a better map of that area and took off for Los Alcázares, where I arrived safely in about an hour. While there at the hotel I met one of my old wing men, Justo García.

There were two other old squadron mates there, too: Riverola, who had gone up to Bilbao, and Alarcón, who had been one of the original members of the *Escuadrilla de LaCalle*. The three of them were getting ready to take the training course for monoplanes. That was the first I had heard about any Spanish pilots being trained for monoplanes, so it was quite interesting. I would have recommended Justo and Riverola any minute for monoplanes, but I was a little doubtful about Alarcón. He had been one of the wing men who had deserted Gómez the day he was shot down on the Guadalajara front and I was a trifle suspicious about the whole affair. But we all had dinner together at the hotel that night and reminisced over the good old days when El Capitán LaCalle had been our guiding light. Incidentally, I found out then that LaCalle had really gone to Russia on a sort of combined health and propaganda trip. He had been receiving a lot of well-earned publicity in Russian newspapers and was touring various Russian cities making lectures, the proceeds of which were being turned over to the Loyalist Government.

The following day Riverola and Justo made their appearance at the hotel and brought along with them one of the original members of the *Escuadrilla de LaCalle,* no other than Gerardo Gil, who had been Whitey's constant companion in the old days. Whitey, Chang, Gil and I had made many a trip to Madrid together. Gil was especially glad to hear that Whitey was only a prisoner, because he knew that no aviators were ever executed; we had too many of Franco's pilots in our own *cárceles* (jails, to you). Gil could hardly believe it when I informed him of the true facts concerning Chang's demise as a Japanese spy. However, the facts were incontrovertible, so there was nothing we could do except throw a binge to celebrate Whitey's escape from what we had thought was a typical aviator's death.

The next day the Russian engineer was back on the job, but it seemed that there were several others ahead of me in line for new planes. He finally told me that the next day I would be given a brand new plane to take back to the front with me. The next morning I loaded myself and my parachute into a car and went out to the field again, where I found monoplane No. 239 waiting for me. But No. 239 soon proved to be even worse than the plane

I had brought down to Los Alcázares with me; as far as the motor was concerned, anyway. Nevertheless, any plane was better than none, so I went to Albacete and then to Alcalá, where I had dinner. I discovered that my squadron was still at Barajas, so I took off again that afternoon and went over there.

On the twenty-ninth of July I made one flight, which turned out to be my last in Spain. Our two red rockets went soaring up over the field house at Barajas, and we climbed to 20,000 feet before deciding that it was a false alarm. The ensuing dive of more than 16,000 feet practically finished the rickety motor with which my plane was equipped. Mechanics swarmed over the plane for the remainder of the day. However, the rest of the squadron made no flights, either, so I didn't miss anything. We were hauled in to Madrid again that night, where we spent another night at the Palace of Fine Arts.

We were being routed out at 4 o'clock in the morning in those days, and were really having to work for our money. During the meal that morning José called up from Alcalá and told me that I was to be sent to Valencia for a few days of rest before the termination of my contract time. A new Russian pilot was sent over to relieve me, and I took him out and showed him the various eccentricities of my plane before turning it over to him. I then celebrated the occasion by going in to Madrid for a hot bath. I returned to Barajas that afternoon just in time to see a most thorough bombardment of my end of the field—by five Junkers. All our planes managed to get off the field in time, however, so no damage was done except to the sod of the field. When I came out of the bomb shelter I collected my baggage and went over to Campo X, where a Ford tri-motored transport plane was waiting. But there were already too many passengers in it when I got there, so I went back to the pilots' house in Alcalá. I was a little glad that I didn't have to leave so soon, anyway, as there were a lot of people I wanted to see before I left.

CHAPTER XVI

HOMECOMING UNDER DIFFICULTIES

I made what turned out to be my last visit to Madrid before leaving Spain. I also stayed in Alcalá two or three more days, but my only journeys were out to the field and over to Campo X, where María and Cristina were again installed in the sewing room of the ex-count's house. That was the only regrettable part of my departure from the Madrid area—leaving those two merry young souls. However, on my last trip over there I took the Victrola along and left it as a parting gift—to cushion what I rather conceitedly thought of as the shock of my departure from their lives. I finally managed to get away from Alcalá on August 5, boarding a truck, with my baggage, at about 4 o'clock in the morning. After about six hours of very rough riding we arrived at the Albacete field just in time for a late breakfast. Fortunately, my old friend General Douglas happened to be there at the time, so I went up to see him after breakfast and he gave me a new Ford V-8 for the remainder of my trip to Valencia.

I had to stay in Valencia for about a week, as I had ordered two suits from one of the local tailors and had to wait for them; but I had no trouble passing the time away. One day I even had the nerve to go up to the American consulate and call on the vice-consul there. That visit was mainly inspired by the thought that I might be able to get a package or two of American cigarettes. From that standpoint the visit was a failure, though, because after repeatedly asking me if I thought there was any danger of the consulate getting bombed, the vice-consul disclosed the fact that he had no cigarettes. I immediately departed, assuring him that he had at least a fifty-fifty chance of not being actually struck by a bomb, but that I was sure the Rebels were going to start using gas bombs very soon. That just about counterbalanced the assurance he gave me that a $1000 fine and three years in jail were the most that I could draw for my activities in Spain.

At Valencia I met Dickenson, who had been with us at Los Alcázares in January. He had failed to pass the examinations for a fighting-plane pilot, but had been accepted as an observation-plane pilot. In the intervening time he had renounced his American citizenship and gone into the regular Spanish Air Force as a provisional captain. He had also married a remarkably good-looking Spanish girl. She had gone to school in New York City and spoke perfect English.

Shortly after leaving Dickenson and his wife I had a pleasant surprise; I met two of my old squadron mates, one of whom I had thought was killed when we were fighting around Guadalajara. It was Manuel Gómez García, accompanied by little Barbeitos, from Coruña. The last time I had seen Gómez was in that dogfight on the Guadalajara front more than four months before. He had certainly had a narrow escape. He had gone into action against five Fiats and had then made the embarrassing discovery that his two wing men were missing. His motor was soon put out of commission and started smoking ominously. He managed to glide into the clouds and then dived for the ground. Just as his wheels touched the ground the entire plane burst into flames; but fortunately the ground was rather rough and the plane somersaulted, throwing him clear of the burning wreckage. He got out of the fight without being struck by any bullets, but his left hand was rather badly burned in that crash landing. He had landed behind the enemy lines and was captured by the Italians. When they found out that he had been piloting one of the planes which had been strafing them they were going to shoot him, but an officer interfered in time to save his life.

He was sent to the military prison at Salamanca after a few days in a temporary jail up at the front. There he was duly tried, sentenced to death, then reprieved, so as to be available for trading purposes. He was kept in prison for more than four months before he was finally traded for one of the Italian pilots we had shot down.

While he was in prison they had fed him just barely enough to keep him alive. When he was finally traded he was hardly able to totter across the lines. His burned left hand was almost useless when I saw him in Valencia. One peculiar thing about our conversation was that it was carried out entirely in Spanish. Gómez had almost forgotten how to speak English, so we found that we could get along better in Spanish. That also gave Barbeitos a chance to understand.

The next morning my two suits were completed and delivered to me at the hotel, so I went down to the Air Ministry and informed Pliny that I was all set to leave. He immediately went to work on my final papers and told me that I would be able to leave the next day for Barcelona. In due time I was in Barcelona taking an afternoon train for Port Bou, on the Franco-Spanish border. The train was crowded but there were several wounded Americans and Canadians aboard, so I was at least able to speak English again. Most of them had been wounded in our recent activities around Madrid.

At 10 o'clock on the morning of Friday the thirteenth we arrived at the little border town of Port Bou, on the Spanish side of the border, where I had undergone my first bombardment some months before. I had no trouble at all getting past the Spanish customs officials, but when we went through the tunnel to Cerbère, on the French side, I again ran into difficulties with my phony passport. The French border guards spoke Spanish with a strong Catalonian accent and I could just barely understand them. I had a perfectly good safe-conduct pass from the Spanish Air Ministry, but it had to have a good passport to go along with it. And those French guards had the effrontery to suspect that I might not be as Spanish as my passport seemed to indicate.

At any rate I was turned over to the French police, who very kindly gave me my choice of either spending the night in the local jail or sleeping on the benches in the railroad station. I had a pretty good idea as to what the local jail would be like, so I chose the station. As I tried to adjust myself comfortably on two wooden benches, placed side by side, I reflected that it served me right for traveling on Friday the thirteenth. I spent most of the night cursing the fiendish skill of the French carpenter who had managed to build the benches so that no two of them were the same height.

The next morning I was taken to Perpignan with an escort of two policemen. There I was taken before the Prefect (same as our sheriff, I believe) for questioning. The Prefect fortunately had an

American wife, and she acted as French-English interpreter. With her assistance I was soon able to convince her husband that I was a real Spaniard, and he gave me a French safe-conduct pass.

When I boarded the train for Paris that afternoon I managed to get into a compartment with three Americans and two Englishmen. The Americans were all returning from the war in Spain. One of them had just finished serving a couple of weeks in the Perpignan jail for failing to have proper papers when he crossed the border. He confirmed my suspicions about French jails. The two Englishmen were on a bicycle tour of France and had decided to save time by going to Paris by train.

We arrived at the Gare d'Orsay at 8:30 the next morning, and I went to the hotel where Baumler was staying. He wasn't in at the time, so I left word for him at the desk and went up to my room for a little rest. That was the first bed I had slept on in four days.

Baumler came up and routed me out about 1 o'clock that afternoon. I noticed that his neck was all bandaged up and, upon inquiring, found that he had left the front none too soon. An infection of certain neck glands had set in, but the doctors were able to operate in time.

Baumler had received a letter from Mrs. Dahl, who was down at Cannes, and she had enclosed a letter that Whitey had managed to send through from Salamanca to her. In his letter Whitey confirmed what the Russian interpreter had told me at Alcalá. He had been captured by Moroccan troops near Brunete and had had a narrow escape from death at their hands. A German officer, however, had intervened and had him sent back to Salamanca, where he was a prisoner in the military hospital. He also said that, aside from being extremely nervous, he was entirely unhurt. However, he failed to state whether he had landed in his parachute or had gone down with his plane. Mrs. Dahl said that she was doing everything she could to try to get her husband released from Spain, but that there was very little chance of her being able to do anything for some time, at least. Baumler and I were glad indeed to hear that Whitey had got down safely, even though he had landed in jail. We both agreed that any man who got shot down twice without getting a scratch was extremely lucky.

After several futile calls at the office of the Spanish representative I managed to find him there, and fixed everything up as far as my Spanish affairs were concerned. By the next day Baumler had completed his plans for getting back to the United States. He was fully equipped with an American passport when he first left the States, but it seemed that there was a little statement in it to the effect that it wasn't valid for travel in Spain. As Baumler had two perfectly legible visas in it showing that he had entered Spain, stayed there seven months and then departed, he thought he had better go back in a somewhat roundabout way. He therefore boarded a Canadian-Pacific liner and set sail from Canada. From there re-entry into the United States proved to be very simple. He merely boarded a transport plane and flew back. My case was not so simple, for I had gone over there as a Spaniard and had nothing but a Spanish passport to do my traveling on. At first I decided to try emigrating to the United States but, as is later shown, I couldn't get away with it.

For the next nine days I was given an excellent demonstration of the inefficiency and snobbery of American consular officials. I tried first to get an American visa on my Spanish passport, but that wouldn't work. The first persons I met after entering the consulate were a couple of naval attachés who had known me back in my naval-officer days, and the game was up. I then made out a formal application for an American passport. I had dabbled a bit in international law and knew that any American citizen who could identify himself as such was entitled to a passport if caught abroad without one—provided, of course, that he wasn't in trouble with the local authorities, which I wasn't.

About three days after making the application I was finally granted an interview with his grace, the vice-consul. I was armed with my naval aviator's identification certificate, with the seal of the United States Navy Department covering both photograph and signature. As it was issued for the express purpose of identification, I was under the impression that it would be sufficient; but not to the vice-consul. He stated that it was insufficient. I then very patiently explained that one had to be an

American citizen to attend the Naval Academy at Annapolis. Still no impression upon the vice-consul. I then suggested that he consult the naval attachés, only two floors above, as to the validity of my certificate and the truth of my statements. I was immediately informed, in an extremely disagreeable tone of voice, that the vice-consul knew how to run his department. And there was nothing at all I could do about it; I needed the passport to get back to the Sates. In fact, I had already had to cancel two steamship tickets on account of the inexcusable delay.

Finally he said that if I could get some American citizen who knew me to identify me, his department would condescend to give me a passport. Baumler had already left for Paris, so I was at a loss as to what to do about it. But luck was again on my side. I went over to Harry's Bar that night and the first person I saw after entering was my old Madrid friend, Ernest Hemingway. When he heard what I needed, he immediately offered to make the required identification. After a few further delays and obstacles I was at last formally identified on August 25 and a passport was made out in my name. It wasn't given to me, though, and I was informed that it would be turned over to the purser of the steamer I was making the crossing in. The steamer would then be met in New York by another set of State Department stooges and they would take charge of the passport. I immediately hied myself over to the French Line offices and managed to get a reservation on the *Champlain*, sailing the following day.

At New York I was met by a State Department representative who had already got my passport from the purser. He asked me various and sundry questions, mostly military ones about late events in Spain. I finally informed him that I had been shell-shocked and would very likely have convulsions or throw a fit if he kept on asking questions which brought back horrible memories. He fell for it and agreed to drop around at a certain hotel that night and get the rest of the information he had been instructed to get. By that time, of course, I was at a very different hotel in Jersey City. I have often wondered if the poor fellow is still poking around in New York hotels trying to "get his man".

Before long, I was motoring from Jersey City down to my

home in Arkansas, and mulling over the memories of the most interesting phase of my life—up to date; thinking how the three remaining members of the American patrol had already scattered. Whitey Dahl was still in prison in Salamanca, after having been sentenced to death and then having the sentence commuted to life imprisonment. Jim Allison was probably somewhere in Old Mexico, although he might be anywhere in the world—you can't tell much about the current whereabouts of a soldier of fortune. And I, once Francisco Gómez Trejo of the *Fuerzas Aéreas Leales*, in seclusion here in the sovereign state of Arkansas, was wondering whether it would take less time to grow a pigtail and travel under a Chinese passport than to try to get an American passport.

In closing I might add that the Spanish Government lived up to, and even above, all the terms of the contract I signed with it. Several disgruntled American pilots returned from Spain claiming that they had been imposed upon; some of them even claiming that they hadn't been paid the amount agreed upon. Every American pilot who went to Spain was given extremely fair treatment, if he carried out his part of the bargain; and even those who couldn't produce were given a full month's pay before being sent back. All in all, I believe I am safe in stating that the Spanish Government treated us much better than our own Government would have done.

For the benefit of those readers who might think it unpatriotic to use training given by this Government in fighting for a foreign Government I will add that I had offered my services to this country long before leaving for Spain. Also, if they care to examine the army files in Washington, they will find that I have lodged another formal offer of my services to the U.S. Army Air Corps since my return. The Air Corps doesn't seem to be interested, however, so I suppose there is nothing left except to follow Horace Greeley's advice and go West.

END

AFTERWORD

by George Nichols

Frank Glasgow Tinker was born in Louisiana in 1909 and spent his childhood in DeWitt, the second largest city in Arkansas County. After graduating from the US Naval Academy in Annapolis he joined the Army Air Corps to train as a pilot, switching back to the Navy Aviation division in 1934. He was discharged the following year after a series of drunken brawls and worked for a while as a third mate on an oil tanker in the Gulf of Mexico.

As he relates in this book, he chose to fly for the Republican Government forces in Spain mainly because he didn't like Mussolini. He was not shy to mention that he also negotiated a very lucrative contract for his services: $1,500 per month and $1,000 bonus for each enemy plane. During his seven months' service in Spain was he credited with shooting down 8 enemy planes, so his total earnings were $18,500 (equivalent to $324,000 in 2019).

Following his return to the US he applied to rejoin both the US Navy and the Army but was rejected by both because of his service in Spain. He wrote articles for various magazines and newspapers, including a series for the Saturday Evening Post under the title *Some Still Live*. These were later collated into this book, which was first published in 1938.

However, the stress of combat and depression at Franco's victory in Spain eventually took their toll. In June 1939 he was found in a hotel room in Little Rock, Arkansas, with a gunshot wound to his head and an empty bottle of whisky beside him, together with a letter of acceptance from the "Flying Tigers" squadron of the Chinese Airforce, to which his friend Baumler had encouraged him to apply. His tombstone was inscribed with the enigmatic epitaph *¿Quién Sabe?* (Who Knows?).

Available direct from *theclaptonpress.com*:

BOADILLA
by Esmond Romilly
As soon as the Civil War broke out in Spain, Esmond
Romilly got on his bike and cycled across France to fight
against fascism. In Boadilla, named after a famous battle in
defence of Madrid, the nephew that Winston Churchill
disowned describes his experiences fighting with the
International Brigade to defend the Spanish Republic.
Written on his honeymoon in France after he eloped with
Jessica Mitford.

MY HOUSE IN MALAGA
by Sir Peter Chalmers Mitchell
While most ex-pats fled to Gibraltar in 1936, Sir Peter
stayed on to protect his house and servants from the rebels.
He ended up in prison for sheltering Arthur Koestler from
Franco's rabid head of propaganda, who had threatened to
'shoot him like a dog'. This is his memoir, written in 1937.

SPANISH PORTRAIT
by Elizabeth Lake
Set principally in San Sebastián and Madrid between 1934
and 1936, this brutally honest, semi-autobiographical novel
portrays a frantic love affair against the backdrop of
confusion and apprehension that characterised the *bienio
negro*, as Spain drifted inexorably towards civil war. It was
described by Elizabeth Bowen as "A remarkable first novel
revealing a remorseless interest in emotional truth".

Available direct from *theclaptonpress.com*:

NEVER MORE ALIVE:
INSIDE THE SPANISH REPUBLIC
by Kate Mangan, with a Preface by Paul Preston
Kate Mangan was a graduate of Slade Art School and
sometime model and danseuse in Paris, much admired by
Augustus John. She went out to Spain in 1936 in search of
her lover, Jan Kurzke, a German refugee who had joined
the International Brigade. She ended up working for the
Republic's Press & Censorship office, travelling around
Spain, visiting the battlefront and meeting a host of
characters including W.H. Auden, Ernest Hemingway,
Robert Capa, Gerda Taro and many others. This is her
previously unpublished memoir

FIRING A SHOT FOR FREEDOM:
THE MEMOIRS OF FRIDA STEWART
with a Foreword and Afterword by Angela Jackson
Frida Stewart campaigned tirelessly to raise funds for the
Republican cause. She drove an ambulance to Murcia, and
visited the front in Madrid. During the Second World War
she was arrested by the Gestapo in Paris and later escaped
from her internment camp with help from the French
Resistance, returning to London where she worked with
General de Gaulle.

BRITISH WOMEN & THE SPANISH CIVIL WAR
by Angela Jackson – 2020 Edition
Angela Jackson's classic examination of the interaction
between British women and the war in Spain, through their
own oral and written narratives. Revised and updated for
this new edition.

CPSIA information can be obtained
at www.ICGtesting.com
Printed in the USA
LVHW021521050322
712646LV00016B/1708